Colonel Theodore Roosevelt

DAVID A. ADLER

Holiday House / New York

For my grandsons,
Jacob, Yoni, Andrew and Aaron

———————————

HOLIDAY HOUSE is registered in the U.S. Patent and Trademark Office.

Printed and Bound in February 2014 at Worzalla, Stevens Point, WI, USA.

www.holidayhouse.com

First Edition

1 3 5 7 9 10 8 6 4 2

Library of Congress Cataloging-in-Publication Data

Adler, David A.

Colonel Theodore Roosevelt / David A. Adler. — First edition.

pages cm

ISBN 978-0-8234-2950-9 (hardcover)

1. Roosevelt, Theodore, 1858–1919—Juvenile literature.

2. Presidents—United States—Biography—Juvenile literature.   I. Title.

E757.A64 2014

973.911092—dc23

[B]

2013018852

President McKinley with Vice President Roosevelt.

PREFACE
Colonel Theodore Roosevelt

Theodore Roosevelt was an explorer, writer, Nobel Prize winner, Lieutenant Colonel with the First Volunteer Cavalry, the Rough Riders, and then a full Colonel. He was an Assemblyman, Police Chief, Assistant Secretary of the Navy, Governor of New York, Vice President, and President. And whatever he did, wherever he served, he was always the center of attention. That suited him. He would not be ignored. Alice Roosevelt said her father "wanted to be the bride at every wedding and the corpse at every funeral."

Theodore Roosevelt had an outsized personality. He was sometimes controversial, often loved, and never dull. He may have been the most talented man of his era. He was surely one of the most interesting.

By 1911, most of his great work was done. He was at his home in Oyster Bay, NY and told his friend the journalist Henry L. Stoddard, "If I were asked what title I prefer it would be Major General in the United States Army in active service. Remember I say active service – no swivel chair for me. Active service, however, is not likely to come in my day," he was already fifty-three years old, "so I suppose 'Colonel' I'll remain to the end. That's good enough." And so when choosing a title for a biography of this multi-talented man, Colonel Theodore Roosevelt seemed fitting.

President Theodore Roosevelt, 1902.

CONTENTS

1. The Cowboy President

It was 1901. The six-month-long Pan-American Exposition, a world's fair, was being held in Buffalo, New York. More than eight million people would come to see the parades, firework displays, staged battles, baseball games, and American Indians demonstrating their War and Ghost dances. Fair visitors would ride a scenic rail-way past Eskimo, African, and Japanese villages, and replicas of a quaint German town and of Venice, Italy, with its gondolas and winding canals. They would see Cleopatra's Temple and get lost in a maze of mirrors called Dreamland. Many of them would travel on an imaginary trip to the moon. One of the fair's most popular attractions was the Upside-Down House. People entered the house through the roof and climbed all the way up to the cellar.

Among the distinguished visitors to the exposition were President and Mrs. William McKinley, arriving in Buffalo by train on Wednesday, September 4. A reported fifty thousand people came to

President William McKinley (1843–1901).

greet them. There was a cannon salute, but in the eagerness to honor the president, workers set one of the big guns too close to the tracks. It blew out several of the train's windows, unnerving Mrs. McKinley.

Leon Czolgosz, a thin twenty-eight-year-old man with dark hair and a round, boyish face, was there on September 4. He was from McKinley's home state of Ohio and seemed especially eager to get close to the president, which alarmed a policeman who shouted at Czolgosz to stand back. Czolgosz quickly blended into the crowd and was gone.

The policeman was right to be frightened. In Czolgosz's pockets were some keys and trinkets, a small amount of money, and a carefully folded year-old newspaper clipping about the 1900 assassination of King Umberto I of Italy by Gaetano Bresci. Bresci was an anarchist; he didn't believe in government. He had traveled from his home in Paterson, New Jersey, to Monza, Italy, to kill the king. Bresci had fired four shots from his .32-caliber Iver Johnson revolver. Three hit the king in the chest, who died immediately. Czolgosz was an anarchist, too, and a would-be copycat assassin. In his pocket was a loaded .32-caliber Iver Johnson revolver.

The next day President William McKinley spoke at the fair. "Expositions are time-keepers of progress," he said. "They stimulate the energy, enterprise, and intellect of the people, and quicken human genius. . . . They broaden and brighten the daily life of the people. . . . Let us ever remember that our interest is in concord, not conflict, and that our real eminence rests in the victories of peace, not those of war."

Leon Czolgosz got to the fair early so he could get close to the president. He pushed his way to the front row, but people kept bumping into him. The president was closely guarded. And before Czolgosz knew it, the speech was done and McKinley was gone.

On Friday, September 6, there was a reception in McKinley's honor in the Temple of Music, a large, ornate yellow building. A Bach sonata was being played on a large organ in a room decorated with screens, flowers, and potted palms. The president stood there

The Temple of Music at the 1901 Pan-American Exposition. The X in the center of the image marks the spot where President McKinley was shot.

and the decor made people meeting him feel as if they were visiting him in his home.

The president was in a cheerful mood. He stood on a slightly raised platform with a large American flag behind him. People came to shake his hand, and he made quick work of it. He reached out, grabbed his visitor's hand, and pulled him slightly toward the exit. This way he could shake more than thirty hands a minute.

The long line of people waiting to meet the president moved forward.

A twelve-year-old girl greeted him and asked for the good-luck flower he had pinned to his lapel. He happily gave it to her.

A tall, foreign-looking man with a black mustache stepped forward. He seemed nervous, which alerted the Secret Service. But the man just shook the president's hand and moved on.

Close behind him was a man wearing a dark suit and string tie. His right hand was wrapped in a handkerchief. Perhaps he had injured it. McKinley reached for the man's left hand but the man never took it. Out of the handkerchief he took a gun, pressed it against the president's chest, and fired twice. McKinley fell. A red stain quickly spread across his white shirt.

"So rapidly was the deed committed," a witness told reporters, "that the police, detectives, soldiers, and everyone stood still without moving a muscle."

McKinley's first thoughts were of his wife and of the man who shot him.

"Be careful how you tell her," he said of his wife.

"Don't let them hurt him," he said of the shooter.

The next man in line, James Parker, an African American, pushed the gunman to the ground. Others piled on top of them.

"I am not badly hurt, I assure you," McKinley told the people standing nearby.

The shooter was quickly taken to the back of the building. "I done my duty," he said.

He said his name was Fred C. Nieman, but it wasn't. He was Leon Czolgosz.

If given the chance, the people at the fair and the people of Buffalo might have killed him. As it was, he was badly beaten by the soldiers and Secret Service men. Keeping him safe until his trial would be a tough challenge for the police.

Czolgosz was taken to Buffalo police headquarters.

The president was rushed to the house of the fair's president, John G. Milburn, which became a mini-hospital. The patient talked to his visitors. He smiled at his doctors. He was doing well.

The day after the shooting it was reported, "The President passed a fairly comfortable night and no serious symptoms have developed." But within a week his condition worsened. He developed a fever. The point where one of the bullets had entered his body became infected. By Friday, September 13, the official report was "The President is sinking."

McKinley's close friend for more than thirty years, Senator

Mark Hanna of Ohio, came to visit. Hanna greeted the president, but McKinley didn't respond.

"William, William, don't you know me?" Hanna cried.

There were tears in the senator's eyes. His hands and head shook in grief.

The president died the next day. His last words were "Good-bye. All good-bye. It is God's way. His will be done, not ours."

A seven-car funeral train took McKinley first to Washington, D.C., and then home to Canton, Ohio. The train was pulled by two engines draped in black cloth followed by seven more cars—a baggage car, a saloon car, and five Pullman sleeper cars. McKinley's coffin rode in the last of the Pullmans. On the train were McKinley's wife, other members of his family, government officials, and reporters.

Senator Hanna was there, clearly distraught by the death of his friend. He was also upset by the prospects for his Republican Party and for the nation. "I told William McKinley it was a mistake to nominate that wild man," he said to the people sitting with him. "Now look, that damned cowboy is president of the United States!"

That "cowboy" had been McKinley's vice president. He was on the train, too. He was Theodore Roosevelt of New York.

Roosevelt certainly didn't look presidential. Historians describe him as "short, nearsighted, beaver-toothed" with "a high pitched voice." But he was confident, smart, and forceful.

In Buffalo, before he took the oath of office, Roosevelt paid his respects to the slain president. He bowed his head and stood quietly by the coffin for several minutes. He was crying openly when he left.

Despite Senator Hanna's misgivings, Roosevelt seemed just right for the office of president. These were busy times, and he was an ever-active man. People described him as a "human steam engine."

This was the beginning of a new century, an era of great challenges.

Almost forty years had passed since the Civil War, but most African Americans still lived in the South and faced widespread discrimination. Many were moving north seeking greater opportunities and freedoms. Civil rights organizations were forming.

In 1900 the average worker was at his job twelve hours a day, six days a week. Many of them were children as young as seven. Each year tens of thousands of workers were killed in on-the-job accidents. There were strikes as workers demanded shorter hours, more pay, and better working conditions.

The nation's population had doubled since 1870. Most people lived in small towns, many without central heating, indoor plumbing, or electricity. Automobiles were new and still called "horseless carriages." The Oldsmobile was the first one built for the masses, but only 425 were made in 1901. People weren't convinced that cars were an improvement over horse-drawn transportation.

Women were expected to wear skirts that reached their ankles, and in all but four states they were not allowed to vote.

The nation was ready for change, and Theodore Roosevelt, the beloved TR, was the man to lead it. Many historians consider him one of our greatest presidents.

2. Teedie

The first Roosevelt to come to America was Klaes Martensen Van Rosenvelt, who came in 1644 to enjoy the freedoms and opportunities of the new Dutch settlement. He traveled in the steerage of a slow-moving boat from Holland and landed in what was then called New Amsterdam and is now Manhattan, one of the five boroughs of New York City. The next seven generations of Roosevelts—the simpler name they adopted in the 1750s—were born in Manhattan.

They had lived there for more than two hundred years when the future president was born on October 27, 1858, in the family home at 28 East Twentieth Street.

By 1858, New York City's population had more than doubled in the past twenty years. It was a "City of Immigrants," especially Manhattan. Two of every three adults living there had been born in some other country.

Many immigrants lived in tenements, apartments in narrow five- to six-story buildings with lots of windowless rooms and no indoor plumbing. The toilets were

East Twentieth Street, the birthplace of Theodore Roosevelt.

trenches dug in the backyards. Musty air mixed with the cooking smells of many traditions filled the poorly ventilated apartments. Clotheslines strung from the windows held drying sheets and undergarments. Wild pigs and rats rummaged in the garbage thrown into the streets and gutters.

The Roosevelt home on East Twentieth Street was just a short distance from those germ-infested neighborhoods, but it was a whole different world. It was a four-story brick and stone house with large, airy rooms including a nursery, a library, and an elegantly furnished front parlor that was used only on Sundays. It had indoor plumbing, and in back was a garden.

Theodore's parents, Martha "Mittie" Bulloch and Theodore "Thee" Roosevelt, were both from wealthy families.

Mittie was born in 1835 and spent her first years in Savannah, Georgia. When she was about five her family moved to Bulloch Hall, a large plantation house her father had built in Roswell, Georgia, just north of the future city of Atlanta. The house had a wide front porch framed by four tall white columns, and overlooked the valley below. Inside it had a high-ceilinged center hall with a grand staircase leading to the bedrooms upstairs. The house had eleven large rooms with a fireplace in each one. It is said to have been the model for Tara, the elegant fictional home in Margaret Mitchell's 1936 best-selling novel *Gone With the Wind*. And just as in Mitchell's book, the Bullochs had slaves to run their house and work in their nearby cotton fields. In all, they had nineteen slaves including a "shadow" or companion slave for each of the children. Black Bess was Mittie's personal slave. She slept on the floor at the foot of Mittie's and her sister Anna's bed.

Mittie was a petite, delicate beauty with what her daughter Corinne described as "black, fine hair" with "moonlight-white" skin. "In the cheeks there was a coral, rather than a rose, tint." She was talkative, loved the outdoors, and was an especially fine horsewoman.

In 1850 a nineteen-year-old visitor came to Bulloch Hall from New York. He was connected to Mittie through a complicated chain of marriages. His brother's wife's brother was married to Mittie's sister. The visitor was Thee Roosevelt. He was handsome and always well dressed. His son Theodore would later describe him as "the finest man I ever knew and the happiest."

Thee was immediately attracted to the petite fifteen-year-old Mittie. They went on walks during the day and read to each other at night. But Mittie was too young to think of a serious relationship, so after a few weeks Thee went home. But he didn't forget her. He sent her a gift, a golden thimble.

For the next three years Thee traveled. He went to the Midwest and Europe. Thee and Mittie met again in 1853 when she came north. She stayed first in Philadelphia and then in New York at the home of Thee's brother, the one whose brother-in-law was married to Mittie's sister. Their love blossomed again, and they were soon married at Bulloch Hall. Following the ceremony was a sumptuous meal with a selection of meats, salads, cakes, and various flavors of ice cream, at the time a rare treat in the South. The Bullochs paid for the extravagant wedding party with the proceeds from the sale of four of their slaves.

The marriage was a match of opposites. Mittie was tiny and delicate and Thee was a large, broad-shouldered man. She was spirited and seemed to live for the moment. He was more careful and disciplined. She was a daughter of the South and he didn't approve of slavery.

After her marriage and move to New York, Mittie's friends found her to be charming but increasingly eccentric. She was obsessed with cleanliness, and each bath she took was really two baths, one to wash, the second to rinse. When she prayed, she would not kneel directly on the floor but on a sheet. To keep the dust out of her hair she kept it in a net. She wore mostly white clothes, but still sometimes it took her so long to decide which white dress to wear that she missed her appointments. She was a fearful woman who suffered from constant nightmares.

In 1855 Mittie and Thee Roosevelt's first child was born, a girl

"Teedie" at age three.

they named Anna and nicknamed Bamie. She was exceptionally smart but unfortunately was born with a deformed spine and needed to wear a steel and leather brace. She was often in pain and needed to lie down. Later she would be devoted to her brother Theodore. During his many years in public life, she was his trusted advisor.

Theodore Jr. was born in 1858. He was nicknamed Teedie. In 1860 Elliot was born and nicknamed Ellie and Nell. In 1861 Corinne was born. She was nicknamed Conie.

The Roosevelts had a fondness for nicknames.

Grandmother Bulloch described Teedie as "sweet and pretty a young baby as I have ever seen." Morris K. Jesup, a family friend, described the young Roosevelt as noisy and fussy.

When Teedie was just two and a half, Southern forces fired on Fort Sumter, a U.S. garrison that guarded the entrance to the harbor in Charleston, South Carolina. With those shots, the Civil War began. The nation was at war with itself. Like the country, the Roosevelts were split. Mittie favored the South. Her brother Irvine was a midshipman in the Confederate navy. Her brother James was an admiral. Mittie's mother and sister Anna left the war-torn South and came to New York. Throughout the war they lived with the Roosevelts.

Thee strongly backed the North, though he didn't enlist. Like many wealthy men of the era, he paid for someone to take his place. Perhaps his eldest son's charge up San Juan Hill as a Rough Rider during the Spanish-American War more than thirty years later was atonement for what he considered his father's cowardice.

Thee visited Union army camps. He spent a lot of time in Washington, where he met with congressmen, socialized with the Lincolns, and, according to his daughter, even helped Mrs. Lincoln shop for hats, giving "his advice on which bonnet was especially

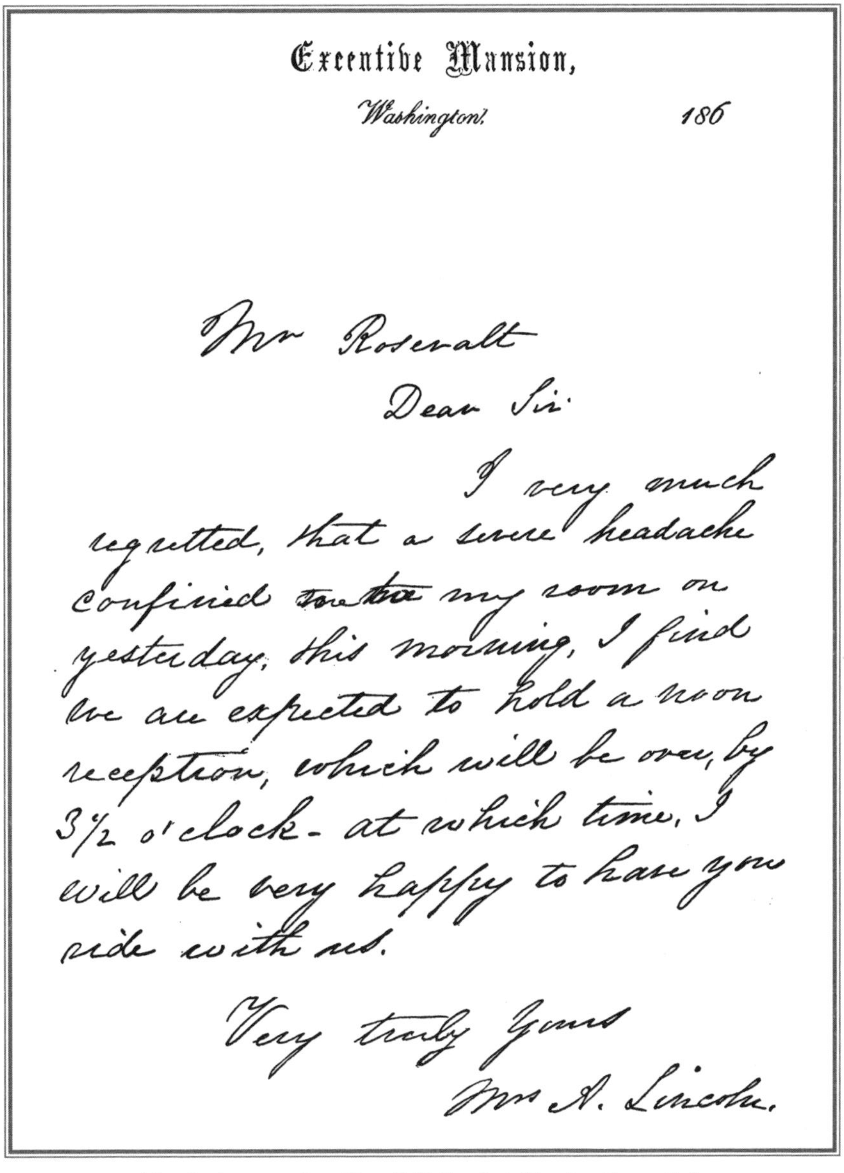

Executive Mansion,
Washington, 186

Mr Roosevelt

Dear Sir:

I very much regretted, that a severe headache confined ~~to the~~ my room on yesterday, this morning, I find we are expected to hold a noon reception, which will be over, by 3½ o'clock - at which time, I will be very happy to have you ride with us.

Very truly Yours

Mrs A. Lincoln.

A handwritten note from Mary Todd Lincoln to Theodore Roosevelt, Sr.

becoming." While he was away, and unknown to him, Theodore and his sister Bamie helped the three Bulloch women give aid to the enemy. They packed boxes with money, medicine, and clothing for Confederate soldiers. Then, in Central Park, the boxes were given to smugglers who somehow got them past the Union lines.

Mrs. Mary Todd Lincoln (1818–1882).

President Abraham Lincoln (1809–1865).

At first the South had major victories, but slowly the tide turned. In the end the Union was preserved, and slavery in the country was eliminated. But more than six hundred thousand soldiers were lost. Many in the defeated South were bitter. On April 14, 1865, a brooding Confederate supporter shot President Lincoln, who died the next day.

On April 25, 1865, six-year-old Theodore Roosevelt watched Lincoln's funeral procession move along New York City's Broadway. With him were his sister Conie and her friend Edith Kermit Carow. Edith would one day be Theodore's second wife.

The wagon that carried Lincoln's body was pulled through the city by sixteen gray horses. An estimated fifty thousand mourners, both blacks and whites, followed it. At first African Americans were to be excluded, but the day before, Secretary of War Edwin Stanton sent a telegram to the city's planning committee. "No discrimination respecting color," he wrote, "should be exercised in admitting persons to the funeral procession."

Forty years later, Secretary of State John Hay would send a locket ring to Roosevelt. Inside the ring's small compartment were some hairs that Hay had cut from Lincoln's head just after he was shot. Hay had been a friend of Lincoln, and at one time was his assistant private secretary. He wanted Roosevelt to wear the ring at his inauguration because TR did "most thoroughly understand and appreciate Lincoln."

"I was a sickly, delicate boy," TR wrote later, "suffered much from asthma, and frequently had to be taken away on trips to find a place where I could breathe." Sometimes, when breathing was especially difficult, his father wrapped him in a blanket and, to force air into his lungs, took him on a wild carriage ride through the city.

"Teedie" at age nine.

Perhaps it was the limits asthma put on him that made him an avid reader. Like many children of his time, he read many of Horatio Alger Jr.'s "rags to riches" stories. Alger's heroes succeeded through a combination of courage, determination, hard work, and honesty, the same principles that would help transform Theodore from a physical weakling to a powerful young man.

When Theodore was twelve, the family doctor suggested that exercising would expand his chest, giving his lungs more room and make it easier for him to breathe. His father remade a room on the second floor of their house into "a kind of open-air gymnasium," his sister Corinne later wrote, "with every imaginable swing and bar and seesaw." Then he told young Theodore, "You have the mind but you have not the body. . . . You must *make* your body. . . ." The little boy looked up and said, "*I'll make my body.*"

Young Theodore was determined. "For many years," his sister wrote, "one of my most vivid recollections is seeing him between the horizontal bars, widening his chest by regular monotonous motion—drudgery indeed—but a drudgery which eventuated in his being not only the apostle but the exponent of the strenuous life."

The gym was open to the outdoors, with just a rail to keep the children from falling out. One day Theodore and his cousin set a wide board on the rail and made a seesaw with one side sticking out over the yard below. "One may well imagine the horror of the mother," Corinne wrote, when she saw Theodore on the overhanging end. "Needless to say, no such feat was ever performed again."

Theodore had constant asthma attacks and hardly ever went to school. Mostly he studied with tutors. His first teacher was his aunt Annie Bulloch. She was a great teller of stories and told him of the Old South, Br'er Rabbit, Daniel Boone, Davy Crockett, and the Bulloch family's role in the American Revolution.

Theodore was a great storyteller, too. When he was just seven or eight, his sister Conie later remembered, "we used to sit, Elliot and I, on two little chairs, near the higher chair which was his, and drink in these tales of endless variety." His stories were always "to be continued." He stretched some stories out for weeks and even months.

Aunt Annie taught Theodore the three R's—reading, (w)riting, and (a)rithmetic. He loved to read and write, but he had almost no interest in the third R, arithmetic. His great interest was in studying wildlife.

"I remember distinctly the first day that I started on my career as zoologist," he wrote in his autobiography. "I was walking up Broadway, and as I passed the market to which I used sometimes to be sent before breakfast to get strawberries, I suddenly saw a dead seal laid out on a slab of wood." He went back day after day to inspect the seal and to measure it. At last he was given the seal's skull, and with two of his cousins started what they called the Roosevelt Museum of Natural History. The museum was housed at home, in the back hall of the second floor.

Among the specimens he kept were live and dead animals. He had a snapping turtle tied to the legs of an upstairs sink, and dead mice in the icebox. There was an entire drawer filled with dead mice, and when his mother ordered a maid to empty it, he mourned "the loss to science." One day he met Mrs. Hamilton Fish, a family friend, on a streetcar, tipped his hat to her, and frogs hopped out. Visitors to the Roosevelt house learned to look before they took a step or a seat.

The Roosevelt children had just about every kind of pet—dogs, cats, rabbits, a racoon, and a pony they named General Grant. During the summer, Corinne later wrote, "We were given great leeway, and were allowed to roam . . . on horseback" or in the water. Corinne also wrote about what she thought was her brother's most striking characteristic.

"He was always reading or writing, and was always able to detach himself from whatever environment he was in and become so absorbed in the book or paper which was the matter on his mind that he was entirely forgetful of what was going on around him. . . . This intense power of concentration," she wrote, "served him well in later life."

As a boy he was interested in the wonders of electricity. "Other boys asked questions," a doctor who knew the young Roosevelt later said. They wanted to know what could be done with electricity. "But Theodore wanted to know the *nature* of the force."

Theodore also loved to hunt. When he was young he went after small game. Later he hunted large game such as elephants, lions, and tigers.

When he was about thirteen he got his first firearm, a quick-loading double-barrel gun. "It puzzled me," he later wrote, "that my companions seemed to see things to shoot at which I could not see at all. One day they read aloud an advertisement in huge letters on a distant billboard, and I then realized that something was the matter, for not only was I unable to read the sign but I could not even see the letters." Soon after that he got his first pair of eyeglasses, which "literally opened an entirely new world" to him.

In May 1869, when Theodore was just ten, he set sail with his family for a year of travel in Europe. He was seasick on the way there and later wrote that he hated the trip, that he didn't think he gained anything from going. However, he did like getting away from his parents and exploring ruins and mountains and playing around in hotels.

Breathing in Europe was no easier for Teedie. He kept a diary during the trip. "I was sick of the Asthma," he wrote in September.

Theodore Roosevelt's "illustrations on the Darwin theory" from a letter to his older sister, 1873.

"I sat up for 4 successive hours, and Papa made me smoke a cigar." (At the time smoking was considered an aid to breathing.)

"In the night I had a nightmare dreaming that the devil was carrying me away," he wrote in October, "but Mama patted me with her delicate fingers."

In November he had another asthma attack, in Paris. "I stayed in the house all day," he wrote, "varying the day with brushing my hair, washing my hands . . . in fact haveing [sic] a verry [sic] dull time." The next day he wrote, "I did the same thing as yesterday."

Throughout the trip, he wrote to Corinne's friend Edith Carow. "We want to get home," he wrote, and "You are my most faithful correspondent. . . . Ever yours, T. Roosevelt."

In May 1870 the Roosevelts returned home, to what the children called "God's country."

Theodore was developing into an odd-looking young man. He was skinny, with long hair, big teeth, and thick eyeglasses. His voice was squeaky and he often smelled of the chemicals he used to preserve his animal specimens.

In October 1872 the Roosevelts returned to Europe. In November they traveled to the Middle East for a two-month cruise on the Nile River in Egypt and a visit to the Holy Land. Theodore later wrote, "This trip formed a really useful part of my education." While traveling on the Nile he shot birds, which he skinned and stuffed. He admitted than his hobby had its dangers. Once, a "well-meaning maid extracted from my taxidermist's outfit the old toothbrush with which I put on the skins the arsenical soap necessary for their preservation, washed it, and left it with the rest of my wash kit." He didn't write whether he ever used the poison-coated brush on his teeth.

"Teedie and Father go out shooting everyday," Corinne wrote in a letter to her aunt. "It certainly is great fun for him." He saw and presumably shot at many birds, including ibis, storks, hawks, owls, pelicans, and doves.

"I think I have enjoyed myself more this winter than I ever did before," he wrote Edith Carow. "Much to add to my enjoyment Father gave me a gun at Christmas. . . . I killed several hundred birds with it."

Many of those birds were first exhibited in the "Roosevelt

Museum." Later they were displayed at Washington's Smithsonian Institution and New York's American Museum of Natural History.

At the beginning of the trip, Theodore and Elliot roomed together. For Elliot that meant staying with his brother's dead birds and mice and the chemicals he used to preserve them. Elliot complained and got his own room.

Corinne wrote of her adventures on the trip. The Roosevelts visited the Temple of Edfu along the bank of the Nile River. "We went into a little dark room and climbed in a hole which was in the middle of the wall. The boys had candles. It was dark, crawling along the passage doubled up. At last we came to a deep hole, into which Teedie dropped, and we found out it was a mummy pit. It didn't go very far in, but it all seemed very exciting to us to be exploring mummy pits."

After their many adventures in the Middle East, the Roosevelts traveled to Europe. Theodore Sr. went to Vienna, Austria, to represent President Grant and the United States at the Vienna Exposition. Theodore Jr. and Elliot were sent to Dresden, Germany, to stay with the Minckwitz family. Dr. Minckwitz was a member of the Reichstag, the German parliament. His wife was a joyful hostess.

In September 1873, in a pithy review of his stay in Germany, Teedie wrote to his sister Anna, "Health; good. Lessons; good. Play hours; bad. Appetite; good. Accounts; good. Clothes; greasy. Shoes; holey. Hair; more 'a-la-Mop' than ever. Nails; dirty in consequence of having an ink bottle upset over them. . . . The other day I much horrified the female portion of the Minckwitz Tribe by bringing home a dead bat."

He also collected rocks. When it was time to leave Dresden, his mother found that he had taken some of his clothes out of his suitcase and replaced them with rocks. When she threw the stones out, he stuffed them into his pockets.

In November 1873 the Roosevelts returned to a different home, a newly built mansion about thirty-five blocks uptown on Fifty-seventh Street.

The other day I much horrified the female portion of the Minork Tribe, by bringing home a dead bat I strongly suspect that they thought I intended to use it as some sorcerer's charm, to injure a foes constitution, mind, or appetite with.

An excerpt from a letter Theodore Roosevelt sent his older sister, Anna, in 1873.

Fifteen-year-old Theodore was now stronger, healthier, and more comfortable meeting new people. His parents decided it was time to prepare him for his next great adventure, college. They wanted him to attend Harvard, but to be admitted he would have to pass the school's difficult entrance exams. To help him study, his parents hired Dr. Arthur Hamilton Cutler. "The young man never seemed to know what idleness was," Cutler wrote later. He studied six to eight hours a day. And when he wasn't studying, he was reading "some English classic, or some abstruse book on Natural History."

Roosevelt easily passed the Harvard exams. In September 1876 he entered the college.

3. As Plain as a Spruce Board

Theodore spent the summer before he entered Harvard on a camping trip in Island Falls, Maine, with Bill Sewall as his guide. He went back three times during school vacations in 1878 and 1879, spending a total of more than two months in the Maine woods.

Sewall was a friendly, strong, and vigorous man, quite a contrast with the thin, pale Theodore Roosevelt, but they got along. "We hitched up well, somehow or other, from the start," Sewall later said. "He was fair-minded, Theodore was. And he took pains to learn everything. There was nothing beneath his notice. I liked him right off. I liked him clear through.... I will say, he wasn't remarkably cautious about expressing his opinion." The people in Island Falls liked him, too. They felt that for a city boy, he didn't put on airs—that he was, as they described him, "as plain as a spruce board and as square as a brick."

TR was almost eighteen years old when he got to college. He wore reddish-brown sideburns, and was of average height but skinny, with a flat chest, narrow shoulders, and wild hair— not yet the rugged-looking man he would become. He was talkative and full of nervous energy. His classmates later said "he was almost the last they would have picked out as a man destined for greatness."

Harvard College is in Cambridge, Massachusetts, just outside Boston. Roosevelt lived off campus in a nearby boarding house, where he kept his animals. Some were alive, including a large turtle and a few harmless snakes, and others were dead and stuffed. Two large Bowie knives hung over the fireplace, and on the mantel was a photograph of his mother. He got around in a sporty, open horse-drawn carriage. To strengthen his legs he skipped rope, at the time a popular pastime among young women but not among men.

Theodore Roosevelt, 1880.

His classmates especially remembered his boxing. He seemed so out of place in the ring, with his spindly legs and thick eyeglasses strapped to his face. What they remembered most was not his fighting, but his sportsmanship. In one match in the school gymnasium in March 1879, the referee called time. Roosevelt dropped his hands and his opponent promptly gave him a mighty wallop. "Foul! Foul!" the onlookers shouted. Roosevelt's face was bloodied, but he wouldn't let the referee punish the other fighter. "He didn't hear!" Roosevelt said. "He didn't hear!" Then he warmly shook the other fighter's hand.

Roosevelt would graduate near the top of his class, but "he was no grind," according to his classmate and lifelong friend William Roscoe Thayer. Roosevelt was not always studying, and he wasn't intent on pleasing his teachers. He often disagreed with them, and held fast to his opinions. Sometimes, according to Thayer, when he should have been studying, he "took long walks and studied the flora and fauna of the country round Cambridge in his amateurish but intense way."

Josiah Quincy was Roosevelt's classmate and in 1895 he would be elected mayor of Boston. His grandfather and great-grandfather, both also named Josiah Quincy, had been mayors of Boston, too. Quincy later remembered that Theodore "showed unusual energy, and the same aggressive earnestness" that he later displayed in public life. "He exhibited a maturity of character, if not of intellectual development, greater than that of most of his classmates." Roosevelt was seen as a man "of determination, pluck, and tenacity."

The title of TR's senior essay was "The Practicability of Equalizing Men and Women Before the Law," quite a forward-looking subject for a student at an all-men's college in 1880. In it he wrote, "I think there can be no question that women should have the equal rights with men . . . especially as regards the laws relating to marriage, there should be absolute equality. . . . *I do not think the woman should assume the man's name.*"

Chester Alan Arthur (1830-1886).

Roosevelt felt he gained a lot from Harvard. "I left college," he later said, "and entered the big world owing more than I can express to the training I had received, especially in my own home; but with much else to learn if I were to become really fitted to do my part in the work that lay ahead for the generation of Americans to which I belonged."

Two life-changing events occurred during Roosevelt's years in Cambridge.

In 1877 President Rutherford B. Hayes nominated Theodore's father to be Collector of the New York Customs House, a major post. Bribes and kickbacks were a regular way of business at the Customs House. The senior Roosevelt's intention was to clean it up. He never got the chance, because future president Chester A. Arthur held the post and refused to step down. In a close vote, taken on December 12, 1877, Roosevelt's appointment was not approved by the Senate. Six days later he collapsed. At first the family thought his political disappointment caused his terrible physical weakness. It hadn't. He had stomach cancer and was "mad with pain," according to his son Elliot.

Theodore Roosevelt Sr. died on Saturday, February 9, 1878. He was just forty-six years old.

Nineteen-year-old Theodore Jr. was heartbroken. "I kissed the dear dead face," he wrote in his diary, "and realized that he would never again on this earth speak to me or greet me with his loving smile."

"What living and loving memories he has left behind him," Roosevelt wrote Corinne a few weeks later. "I can *feel* his presence sometimes when I am sitting alone in the evening . . . there are every now and then very bitter moments."

Theodore's second life-changing event came half a year later, when at the home of his friend Richard Saltonstall he met seventeen-year-old Alice Hathaway Lee. She had curly, light brown hair, blue eyes, and a slightly upturned nose, and at five feet seven inches, she was almost as tall as Roosevelt. "I saw her sweet, fair young face," Roosevelt later remembered, and he was in love.

Roosevelt told her about his turtles and snakes. He talked on and on. During school breaks, when they were apart, he wrote her long letters. He gave her expensive gifts. "See that girl?" he said at a party to a friend, and pointed to Alice. "She won't have me, but I'm going to have her." He said, "I'm going to marry her."

He did.

Theodore Roosevelt and Alice Hathaway Lee were married at First Parish Church in Brookline, Massachusetts, on October 27, 1880, Roosevelt's twenty-second birthday.

Mrs. Alice Hathaway Lee Roosevelt (1861–1884).

From the church, the wedding guests went to a reception in nearby Chestnut Hill, at the home of the bride's parents. Among those celebrating was Edith Carow, Roosevelt's childhood friend, who seemed happy for Theodore. According to reports, she "danced the soles off her shoes."

During the summer of 1881 he and his wife went on a belated honeymoon. They traveled through Italy, Switzerland, Germany, France, and England. The boat trip wasn't an easy one for the young bride, who was seasick almost the entire way across the Atlantic. "I fed her every blessed meal," Roosevelt wrote in a letter, "and held her head when, about 20 minutes later, the meal came galloping up into the outer world again."

Sometime in 1880, just before he left the Boston area, Roosevelt had gone to his doctor for a checkup. His doctor told him he had heart trouble, that he should be careful not to exert himself. He should not even run up a flight of stairs.

Despite his doctor's warnings, while on his honeymoon TR climbed two of the highest mountains in the Swiss Alps, the Jungfrau and the Matterhorn. The Matterhorn already had a tragic history for climbers. It had first been conquered in 1865, just sixteen years earlier, and four members of the first team to reach its summit fell to their deaths on their way down. When Roosevelt reached England, in recognition of his climbs he was made a member of the Alpine Club of London.

The young couple went to live with Roosevelt's widowed mother in New York City. At meals TR was given his late father's seat at the head of the table. He also took his father's place on the boards of many of the charitable institutions he had supported.

After his graduation from college, Roosevelt studied at Columbia Law School. He was a good law student. He took lots of notes, and according to Professor Burgess, one of his teachers, he "seemed to grasp everything instantly." But he wasn't destined to be a lawyer. "Some of the teaching of the law books and of the classroom seemed to me against justice," he later wrote. He was surrounded with people who looked up to big corporation lawyers and who, according to Roosevelt, "held certain standards which were difficult to recognize as compatible with the idealism I suppose every high-minded young man is apt to feel."

Later, when he was in government, he attacked some of those corporations.

While at Columbia, Roosevelt gave a lot of thought to his future. He believed "a man's first duty is to pull his own weight" to support his wife and family, "but it happened that I had been left enough money by my father not to make it necessary for me to think solely of earning bread . . . while I must earn money, I could afford to make earning money the secondary instead of the primary object of my career."

In September 1881 Roosevelt started his second year of law school. He also attended his first political meeting.

TR later remembered that when he asked about the local political club, his friends laughed at him. They told him that "politics were 'low'; that the organizations were not controlled by 'gentlemen,' " but by "saloon-keepers, horse-car conductors, and the like."

Roosevelt had decided to join the "governing class," and if the others in politics "proved too hard-bit" he would have to quit. But, he said, "I certainly would not quit until I had made the effort and found out whether I really was too weak to hold my own in the rough and tumble."

In 1882, before graduating, Roosevelt left law school. He had found his life's work. He would enter politics.

4. "My Heart's Dearest"

The Republican Club of New York's Twenty-first Assembly District met in a large open room above a saloon on Fifty-ninth Street, a short walk from Roosevelt's home. The room was furnished with a table in front, some chairs and benches, and scattered about the room were spittoons—brass bowls for the spit of obviously careless tobacco chewers. Proof of their carelessness were the many tobacco juice stains on the floor around each spittoon. On the wall was a portrait of President Ulysses S. Grant.

"I joined," Roosevelt said later, "attended the meetings, and did my part in whatever was going. We didn't always agree and sometimes they voted me down and sometimes I had my way. They were a jolly enough lot and I had a good time."

Throughout his life, the loud and opinionated Roosevelt was seldom "lost in a crowd," and in 1881, when it came time to pick a candidate for the New York State Assembly from the city's Twenty-first District, the leaders of the club chose him. It was a mostly Republican district, and he won easily. At twenty-three he was the youngest member of the state legislature, which met in Albany, the capital. Ike Hunt, a fellow assemblyman, described Roosevelt as impulsive and "the most indiscreet guy I ever met." He was reelected in 1882 and in 1883.

Jay Gould (1836–1892).

On April 5, 1882, during his first term, he called for a resolution for an investigation of Judge Theodore Westbrook, who was tied to the powerful newspaper owner and industrialist Jay Gould. TR called Gould a "swindler" and said that the people of New York should have judges who were "beyond reproach." The *New York World*, an influential newspaper owned by Gould, strongly objected to the resolution. But in the end, by a lopsided final count of 104 to 6, the assembly voted to look into TR's allegations of corruption. At first it seemed Roosevelt had won, but he hadn't. The investigation concluded that at times the judge might have been "unwise," but he wasn't crooked.

The assembly was only part-time work. In 1882 Roosevelt joined the New York National Guard, and he was quickly promoted to captain. Also that year, his first book, *The Naval War of 1812*, was published to good reviews. According to the *New York Times*, the book was "an excellent one in every respect." The newspaper declared that Roosevelt "showed in so young an author the best promise for a good historian—fearlessness of statement, caution, endeavor to be impartial, and a brisk and interesting way of telling events."

His work in the assembly did not always go well. On many issues he was, in his words, "absolutely deserted." But he was learning. "That was my first real lesson in politics," he said later. "It was just this; if you are cast on a desert island, with only a screw driver, a hatchet, and a chisel to make a boat with, go make the best you can. It would be better to have a saw, but you haven't. So with men. There is a point of course where a man must take his stand alone and break with all for a clear principle, but until it comes, he must work with men as they are."

Beyond his work, he had a busy personal life.

Shortly after his wedding, Roosevelt bought ninety-five acres on Long Island's North Shore, in Oyster Bay. He hired architects and

The Roosevelt home in Oyster Bay, N.Y. Roosevelt later named the house "Sagamore Hill."

told them to draw plans for a ten-bedroom house. Surely with all those bedrooms he hoped to have lots of children.

In the early summer of 1883 there was good news. Alice Roosevelt was pregnant.

"I am so delighted," Alice wrote in a letter.

Surely TR also was pleased. Nonetheless, he decided he needed to get away. His asthma had returned, along with severe stomach pains. He decided to go west, breathe clean air, and hunt buffalo.

In September he traveled west by train for five days, more than two thousand miles to the Dakota Territory, to a town known as Little Missouri. Fewer than one hundred people lived in Little Missouri, and none of them were lawmen. Disputes there were settled with guns.

That was fine with TR.

Roosevelt hired a guide named Joe Ferris, and for more than a week they rode together in search of a buffalo herd. At first they found adventure of a different sort. Roosevelt was on the ground trying to sneak up on an antelope when he heard the rapid rat-a-tat of a rattlesnake. "We shot him and took his rattles," TR wrote to his wife.

Theodore Roosevelt in hunting clothes, 1885.

On the hunt, TR's horse got trapped in quicksand and had to be rescued. Then one night their horses were spooked and ran off. Roosevelt and Ferris chased after them. When they caught the horses, they returned to camp exhausted. While they slept, it rained. The two hunters woke up in four inches of water.

"By Godfrey, but this is fun," Roosevelt told his guide.

At last they found fresh buffalo tracks.

"I dismounted at once," Roosevelt wrote to his wife, and he followed the tracks. "I caught sight of him feeding at the bottom of a steep gulley; I crawled up to the edge, not thirty yards from the great, grim looking beast, and sent a shot from the heavy rifle into him just behind his shoulder. . . . He dropped dead before going a hundred yards." He ended his letter with "a thousand kisses for you, my own heart's darling I am ever your loving, Thee."

Roosevelt loved the Wild West and intended to come back, so before he left he gave his guide's brother and another man money to buy a large herd of cattle for him and to look after them. He would later buy two ranches in the Little Missouri area, one named the Maltese Cross and the other the Elkhorn Ranch.

He returned to New York with the head of the buffalo he shot and the antlers from two stags. He was back in time to serve his third term in the New York State Assembly in Albany.

Roosevelt found corruption in the New York City sheriff's office and in the vermin-infested jails. There were bugs in the food and

Roosevelt's Elkhorn Ranch house.

William "Boss" Tweed (1823–1878).

not enough water for washing. Prisoners were expected to bribe the guards for decent cells. One prisoner at Ludlow Jail who had made himself very comfortable was William "Boss" Tweed, the infamous Democratic leader and the man behind the building of a New York City courthouse that was said to have cost more than the recent U.S. purchase of the entire territory of Alaska. Tweed had been convicted for stealing millions of dollars from the city, but he was living well in jail. He reportedly paid seventy-five dollars a week to live in the warden's parlor.

Roosevelt worked to end corruption and improve conditions at Ludlow.

On Tuesday night, February 12, 1884, there was good news for Roosevelt. His wife had given birth to a healthy girl. He left Albany and happily boarded a train bound for New York City. He arrived late the next night to find that the good news had turned tragic. His brother Elliot met him at the door. "Mother is dying and Alice is dying, too," he said. Their mother had typhoid fever. Alice had a kidney ailment—Bright's disease. "There is a curse on this house," Elliot said.

Roosevelt hurried to his wife. He held her, but she hardly recognized him. After a couple of hours he went to his mother's bedside. Just six years earlier, Roosevelt's father had died in that same room. Roosevelt went from one bedside to the other. His mother died first, and a short time later his wife, Alice, died, too.

Roosevelt repeated his brother's words: "There is a curse on this house."

His mother was just fifty years old.

His wife was only twenty-two.

At 10 A.M., on Saturday, February 16, 1884, there was a double funeral at Fifth Avenue Presbyterian Church. The church was crowded with relatives and friends. Many of them cried as the family's longtime pastor, the Reverend Dr. John Hall, delivered a brief eulogy for the two women. Then they stood with their heads bowed as the two rosewood coffins covered with wreaths of lilies, roses, and vines were carried past them to the two horse-drawn hearses waiting outside. The burial was in Greenwood Cemetery in Brooklyn.

Roosevelt's former teacher Dr. Cutler described TR as "dazed" and "stunned" through the funeral and burial. "He does not know what he does or says."

A year later Roosevelt wrote of his wife Alice, "She was beautiful in face and form, lovelier still in spirit; as a flower she grew, and as a fair young flower she died. . . . And when my heart's dearest died, the light went from my life for ever."

The day after the funeral Roosevelt's daughter was christened Alice Lee, but her father called her Baby Lee. Even the mention of the name Alice was painful to him. On a chain around Baby Lee's neck was a locket, and inside it was a lock of her mother's hair.

Roosevelt left his daughter with his sister Bamie.

He hardly spoke of his late wife again.

Police Commissioner Roosevelt at his desk.

5. Assemblyman, Rancher, Police Commissioner, Navy Man

"It was a grim and evil fate," Roosevelt wrote after the sudden deaths of his wife and mother. But he added, "I have never believed it did any good to flinch or yield for any blow, nor does it lighten the blow to cease from working."

On Monday, February 18, just two days after the double funeral of his wife and mother, Theodore Roosevelt returned to his work in Albany and was busier than any other member of the assembly. He wrote bills and held hearings both in Albany and in New York City. He helped pass laws to end corruption in New York government.

In June 1884 he was a delegate to the Republican National Convention in Chicago. Party leaders supported James G. Blaine, former speaker of the House of Representatives, senator, and secretary of state. But Roosevelt didn't trust him. He fought against Blaine's nomination and made some powerful enemies including Roscoe Conkling, a former senator from New York, who called TR "that dentificial young man with more teeth than brains."

Despite Roosevelt's efforts, Blaine won the nomination.

Roosevelt didn't go home after the convention. He went farther west, to his ranch in the Dakota Territory. He went there with a pile of books and his handsomely engraved rifle. Although he was a bit stuffy and insisted on being called "Mr. Roosevelt," to the Dakota cowboys he was okay.

"I do not believe there ever was any life more attractive to a vigorous young fellow than life on a cattle ranch," he wrote in 1913. "It was a fine, healthy life, too; it taught a man self-reliance, hardihood, and the value of instant decision."

Many years later he wrote, "We led a free and hardy life with horse and rifle." He wrote of the "scorching midsummer sun," the "freezing misery" of the fall cattle roundups, and the "blinding blizzards" of winter. "But," he wrote, "we felt the beat of hardy life in our veins, and ours was the glory of work and the joy of living."

TR was busy from early morning until nightfall. He spent much of that time in the saddle, riding among his cattle and chasing after runaway horses. And the horses he rode weren't always docile. One threw him onto a rock and broke his arm. Another horse fell backward on Roosevelt and injured his shoulder. The nearest doctor was more than one hundred miles away, so there was nothing for TR to do but get back in the saddle.

"The only time I ever had serious trouble," he wrote in his autobiography, was in the barroom of a small hotel. "A shabby individual in a broad hat with a cocked gun in each hand was walking up and down the floor." The other five or six men in the room kept out of his way. Then Roosevelt walked in.

"Four-eyes!" the man shouted because of Roosevelt's eyeglasses.

The others in the room laughed.

"Four-eyes is going to treat!" the man shouted, expecting Roosevelt to pay for all the men's drinks.

"He stood leaning over me, a gun in each hand, using very foul language," Roosevelt later remembered. "His heels were close together, so that his position was unstable." Roosevelt got up and quickly punched him in the face three times. The man's head hit the corner of the bar. "He was senseless." The others carried him out to a shed. When he awoke, he hurried to the train station and left town.

Roosevelt could not be bullied, but he was not fearless.

"There were all kinds of things I was afraid of at first," he later wrote, "ranging from grizzly bears to 'mean' horses and gunfighters; but by acting as if I was not afraid I gradually ceased to be afraid."

When there was a break in his work at the ranch, he and a guide went on Rocky Mountain hunting trips. "We would follow the tracks by the slight scrapes of the claws on the bark, or by bent and broken twigs," he wrote of one bear hunt. "We advanced with noiseless caution, slowly climbing over dead trunks and upturned stumps . . . and there, not ten steps off, was the great bear, slowly rising from his bed among the young spruces. . . . Then he saw us, and dropped down again on all fours, the shaggy hair on his neck and shoulders seeming to bristle as he turned to us." Roosevelt raised his rifle and shot the bear between the eyes.

At times he was foolhardy. Once, he had his guide hold him by his feet over the edge of a cliff so he could shoot a picture of a mountain lion. He was hanging head down two hundred feet above an icy stream, and when it was time to pull TR up, the men he was with found they just couldn't do it. So one of the men went back to their camp, got some more rope, and lowered TR until he was thirty-five feet above the water. There was no more rope, so they dropped TR. After his fall, he was woozy, bruised, and shivering, but he didn't complain.

Roosevelt spent most of 1884–1886 in the Dakotas, but he did return several times to New York to visit with his daughter, Alice, to connect with his political colleagues, and to see his childhood friend Edith Carow.

In September 1886, soon after TR returned to New York, at the insistence of leaders of the city's Republican Party he became the party's candidate for mayor. He had little chance of winning, but win or lose, he was back in politics. He pledged to be honest in office. Nonethless, he came in third in a three-way race.

Just a few days after the election, Roosevelt and his sister Bamie

Edith Kermit Carow Roosevelt (1861–1948).

sailed to England. For more than a year TR had been secretly engaged to Edith Carow. She was in London now, and on December 2, at St. George's Church, they married.

In a 1915 letter he described himself as "a gouty old man" and Edith as "pretty and charming."

"I have tremendous admiration for her judgement," Roosevelt said of Edith. "She is not only cultured but scholarly." She has been described by many as "the love of his life."

The walls of their house in Oyster Bay were covered with dark wood panels. It was decorated with Roosevelt's hunting trophies—animal skins, heads, and antlers. It seemed a real "man's house," but it was ruled by a woman. Edith made all the family and household decisions.

Edith and Theodore's first child together, Theodore Roosevelt Jr., was born the next year. There were four more Roosevelt children: Kermit, Ethel, Archibald, and Quentin.

All was not tranquil in the Roosevelt household. TR's children with Edith did not fully accept Alice, Roosevelt's daughter from his first marriage. They taunted her, constantly reminding her that she was just a half sister. Alice later remembered, "They were very cruel about it and I was terrible sensitive."

Alice found solace with her maternal grandparents, who spoiled her. They gave her new clothes and extravagant gifts including a pony. Roosevelt told his wife they'd better be nice to Alice: "We might have to ask her for money."

While Roosevelt was in New York and London, the people in

the Dakota Territory suffered through the terrible winter of 1886–1887. The temperature fell to more than forty degrees below zero. Snow kept falling until it was four feet deep, and snowdrifts were even deeper than that. In March, when the snow and ice finally melted, there were floods. And in the rushing water were the bodies of dead cattle. More than half of Roosevelt's herd was gone. He was soon out of the cattle business.

TR had lost tens of thousands of dollars in his failed attempt at ranching. He turned to writing to earn money. In the next few years several of his books were published, including biographies of Senators Thomas Hart Benton of Missouri and Gouverneur Morris of New York and a four-volume set titled *The Winning of the West*.

The Roosevelts were now living in their new twenty-two-room house in Oyster Bay, Long Island, a house they later named Sagamore Hill. On the third floor was TR's gun room, with souvenirs from the Dakotas and a desk where he did his writing.

"I shall probably never be in politics again," he told a friend.

He was wrong.

In 1888 Republican Benjamin Harrison was elected president. He appointed Roosevelt as one of three civil service commissioners. In 1877 TR's father had planned to clean up the New York Customs House. Now TR planned to clean up the civil service.

Just four years earlier, in 1884, Grover Cleveland, a Democrat, had been elected president, the first of his party since before the Civil War. After the election his vice president, Thomas A. Hendricks of Ohio, said he would "take the boys in out of the cold to warm their toes." He did. Lots of them got government jobs—they warmed their toes by the government's fireplace.

President Grover Cleveland (1837–1908).

Roosevelt as Police Commissioner from an 1880s Harper's Weekly *cartoon.*

Roosevelt was intent on ending this practice of paying off political debts with government jobs. He and his fellow commissioners controlled many jobs in the civil service. Under his leadership workers were now hired based on merit. Applicants who scored highest on a competitive exam got the job.

In 1895 Roosevelt brought his passion for clean government closer to home. He resigned from the civil service to become one of New York City's police commissioners. Before he joined the force, men had to pay bribes of hundreds of dollars to be appointed policemen, and thousands more to be promoted. They got their money back by blackmailing criminals. Roosevelt stopped all of that.

While he was commissioner a newspaper reporter went to see Roosevelt. "I saw a steady stream of men going up and down stairs, which led to the second floor of police headquarters. It was the crowd which moves in and out of Mr. Roosevelt's rooms all day long." The reporter added, "Theodore Roosevelt is the biggest man in New York to-day."

But he didn't just sit behind his desk. Late at night he put on a dark cloak and a large, wide-brimmed hat that hid his face, and walked through the streets checking on his men.

One night he found a policeman standing by the entrance to a saloon and drinking a beer. The man ran off, but Roosevelt caught him.

Another night he found one of his men sitting by his post socializing. When the policeman followed him to explain, Roosevelt told him that now he was off his post. "Go back to your beat, now." He would speak to him in the morning.

During his two years as commissioner, it was a joke among New Yorkers that police were always on the lookout for someone in a dark cloak with thick eyeglasses and large, shiny teeth. His raids became so talked about that street peddlers sold toy whistles made in the form of "Teddy's Teeth." Roosevelt said the toys were "very pretty."

"Did the police hate Roosevelt for making them do their duty?" the journalist Jacob Riis later wrote. "No, they loved him." Riis accompanied Roosevelt on many of his walks through the tougher sections of the city. Riis added that the great majority of the men on the force were good and true and were glad to have a strong, honest boss.

Police Commissioner Roosevelt.

"These midnight rambles are great fun," TR wrote to his sister. "I get a glimpse of the real life of the swarming millions."

While he was police commissioner, his commonsense approach often defused difficult situations.

Dr. Hermann Ahlwardt, a German agitator and notorious anti-Semite, was coming to the city and wanted police protection for one of his meetings. Others insisted that he not be allowed to speak. "Of course I told them," Roosevelt said, "that the right of free speech must be

Jacob Riis (1849–1914).

maintained." TR had another idea. He told one of his associates, "Select thirty good, trusty, intelligent Jewish members of the force, men whose faces clearly show their race, and order them to report to me." Roosevelt assigned those officers to guard Ahlwardt. They stood "mute and stiff as statues," but having them there ruined the agitator's meeting.

While Roosevelt was on the job, bicycle policemen were added to the force. His officers distributed thousands of blocks of ice during an August 1896 heat wave. He opened a gun-shooting school for his men. But his best-known and probably least-popular work as commissioner was his enforcement of the law that prohibited the sale of liquor on Sunday. To Roosevelt, his duty was clear. "I would rather see this administration turned out because it enforced the laws," he said, "than see it succeed by violating them."

In 1896 TR moved on to another job. William McKinley, a Republican and the former governor of Ohio, was elected president. He appointed Roosevelt, the author of the definitive naval history of the War of 1812, to be assistant secretary of the Navy. TR's immediate goal was to make the nation a naval power in both the Atlantic and Pacific oceans. He believed the best way to guarantee peace was to be prepared for war. "No nation can hold its place in the world," he said, "or can do any work really worth doing, unless it stands ready to guard its rights with an armed hand." But he found the Navy unprepared to protect the country. In 1898 it had just ninety ships, and more than half of them were either not water-ready or out of commission.

Roosevelt petitioned Congress for ships, guns, and ammunition. He had to go from one board to the next to make his requests. "Gentlemen," he finally said in desperation, "if Noah had been obliged to consult such a commission as this about building the ark," he would still be going to meetings.

At the time, there was mischief in the waters off the coast of Florida. People of the nearby island of Cuba were in open rebellion against Spanish rule. Then on February 15, 1898, there was a horrendous explosion in Cuba in the Havana harbor. Without any warning, the U.S. battleship Maine was blown out of the water. More than two hundred fifty sailors and officers were killed. Rumors spread that Spain was guilty of the attack.

President McKinley appointed a board of inquiry to look into the cause of the disaster, but the editors of popular newspapers didn't wait for its findings. "FOUL PLAY!" declared one paper. Another blamed the explosion on "AN ENEMY'S INFERNAL MACHINE." "Remember the Maine!" became the nation's battle cry.

Near the end of March the report was in. An "external explosion" had destroyed the Maine. Though it did not identify who was responsible, the American people blamed Spain. By April the United States was at war.

A few weeks later Roosevelt told a friend, "Everybody in Washington whose opinion I respect . . . think I can be of more service by remaining at my post in the Navy Department, but I have always said if my country ever engaged in war, I should take part." He told his friend, "I leave for the front tomorrow."

Colonel Roosevelt and his Rough Riders atop San Juan Hill, 1898.

6. Rough Rider, Governor, Vice President

Even during peacetime, Theodore Roosevelt was eager to put on a soldier's uniform. In 1897 he wrote, "Every man who has in him any real power of joy in battle knows that he feels it when the wolf begins to rise in his heart; he does not shrink from blood and sweat . . . he revels in them, in the toil, the pain, and the danger."

In 1898, when the United States went to war with Spain, TR and his friend Leonard Wood, a physician who had fought in the Indian wars, formed the First United States Volunteer Cavalry. Roosevelt was given the rank of lieutenant colonel. Wood was made a colonel. Their plan was to recruit a regiment of one thousand cowboys, foxhunters, and other experienced horsemen. The men had to be in good health, know how to ride and shoot, and be willing to obey orders.

"We drew recruits from Harvard, Yale, Princeton, and many another college," TR later wrote. "I had such a swarm of applications from it that I could not take one in ten." More than twenty-three thousand men had volunteered.

Rough Rider Roosevelt.

Roosevelt and Wood chose a varied group. Among them were four policemen who had served under Roosevelt in New York City, the Harvard football team quarterback, a champion tennis player, a steeplechase rider, a polo player, Roosevelt's friend and Dakota ranch partner Robert Munro Ferguson, cowboys from New Mexico, Arizona, and Oklahoma, hunters, a mining prospector, and some American Indians. Many had colorful nicknames including Happy Jack of Arizona, Rattlesnake Pete, Cherokee Bill, Smokey Moore the broncho buster, Tough Ike, Metropolitan Bill, and a Jewish soldier was nicknamed Pork Chop. Like their leaders Roosevelt and Wood, they were all patriots and adventurers.

At first people playfully called the troop "Teddy's Terrors." That name didn't stick. "Rough Riders" did. They were called that because many cowboys and "rough-and-ready Westerners" had joined the regiment.

The troop met and trained in San Antonio, Texas. On May 29, 1898, they left for Tampa, Florida, and from there sailed to Cuba. On July 1 TR led his men on an assault of Kettle Hill. Once that was taken, they advanced to the Spanish stronghold of San Juan Hill. They were joined in the attack by the Ninth Cavalry, an African-American regiment. Roosevelt waved his hat and both regiments followed him.

Richard Harding Davis, a reporter for the *New York Herald*, was there. "The men held their guns pressed against their breasts and stepped heavily as they climbed," he wrote. "They walked to greet death at every step, many of them, as they advanced, sinking suddenly or pitching forward and disappearing in the high grass. . . . It was a miracle of self-sacrifice, a triumph of bulldog courage."

There were heavy losses. More than one

Richard Harding Davis (1864–1916).

Theodore Roosevelt in Rough Rider uniform, 1898.

hundred thirty of Roosevelt's men were injured, killed, or overcome by the heat. "We had a bully fight at Santiago," TR later wrote. "Frankly, it did not enter my head that I could get through without being hit, but I judged that even if hit the chances would be about three to one against my being killed; that was the proportion of dead to wounded here."

Two weeks later the Spanish signed a treaty of peace. They gave up their dominion over Cuba, the Philippine Islands, and Puerto Rico.

The Rough Riders returned to Montauk Point, at the eastern tip of Long Island. On the Sunday before they disbanded, Roosevelt was visited by the entire troop. One of the men presented him with a gift, a two-foot-high bronze sculpture by the Western artist Frederick Remington. "Outside of my own immediate family," he told the men, "I shall always feel that stronger ties exist between you and me than exist between me and anyone else on earth." He shook each man's hand and thanked him for the gift and his service.

Roosevelt was true to his word. For the rest of his life, he was always ready to meet with the men who had served with him as Rough Riders, and whenever they needed help, he was there for them. When TR was president, Senator Shelby M. Cullom of Illinois came to see him and was told he'd have to wait. Roosevelt was busy with another visitor.

"Who is in there?" Cullom asked. When he was told it was a former Rough Rider, he left. "What chance have I," he said, "merely a senator?"

According to his college classmate William Roscoe Thayer, when Rough Rider Colonel Theodore Roosevelt returned to Long Island, he "was the most popular man in America."

Leaders of the New York Republican Party took notice. They greeted Roosevelt on his return and convinced him to be their candidate for governor.

It was a close election. When Roosevelt went to bed at ten o'clock on Election Night, he thought he had lost. Four hours later a group of celebrating supporters woke him. He came to the door in a pair of red pajamas and learned he was the newly elected governor of New York. The margin of victory was just over 1 percent of the 1,350,000 votes cast.

Roosevelt still had a passion for clean government. He refused to listen when Republican Party bosses told him whom to appoint to important state positions. Instead he chose the most qualified, able people he could find for the jobs. And, despite the political bosses' opposition, he raised taxes on rich corporations. TR also enforced the Factory Law, which improved working conditions in New York City's infamous sweatshops.

"I am proud of being governor," Roosevelt wrote in a letter to his friend from Maine, Bill Sewall. "I do not expect, however, to hold political office again, and in one way that is a help, because the politicians cannot threaten me."

For New York Republican Party leaders his independence had become a problem. One party boss complained that TR "did just what he pleased." What could be done with Roosevelt? The people of New York loved him. If he ran again, he would surely win.

In 1900 President McKinley was also up for reelection, and there

As governor of New York, (1899–1900).

was an opening on his ticket. Vice President Garrett A. Hobart had died in November 1899. A rumor quickly spread that McKinley would choose Roosevelt as his running mate.

The bosses in New York were for it. "I don't want him raising hell in my state," one boss declared. "I want to bury him." And the office of vice president seemed an ideal burying ground, a mostly ceremonial job in the shadow of a popular president.

McKinley's good friend and adviser Senator Mark Hanna of Ohio was against it.

Even Roosevelt was against it. "Under no circumstances," he said, "could I or would I accept the nomination for the Vice-Presidency."

But the delegates at the Republican National Convention over-whelmingly wanted him. They cheered wildly when he was nomi-

Senator Mark Hanna of Ohio trying to control vice presidential candidate Roosevelt.

William Jennings Bryan (1860–1925).

nated. They held up signs and banners. They threw their hats into the air. The band played but could hardly be heard over the shouts of the crowd. And when the votes were counted, all but one was for Roosevelt. TR had not voted for himself; he wasn't even in the hall. He was in a room nearby reading a book by Thucydides, the ancient Greek historian.

"I had to take it," he told his friend and pastor Dr. Iglehart shortly after the convention. "I protested against the nomination, sincerely and vehemently . . . I repeatedly refused to accept it. . . . But, Doctor, I had to do so. If I had not, the people of this country would never have given me another office worth while, as long as I live."

"We have the best ticket ever presented," Senator Depew of New York told the convention, "the statesman and the cowboy. The accomplished man of affairs and the heroic fighter. The man who has proved great as president, and the fighter who has proved great as governor."

Once nominated, TR accepted his role and campaigned throughout the country. He traveled more than twenty thousand miles by train to twenty-four states, and made almost seven hundred speeches in almost six hundred towns to three million people.

Between campaign stops, Roosevelt rested his voice and read one of the many books he had brought along. Among them was a collection of brief biographies of ancient men by the Greek historian Plutarch. He kept that book in one of his coat's side pockets and read from it each day he traveled. "I've read this little volume close to a thousand times," he once said, "but it is ever new."

The big issue of the campaign was the gold standard. At the time, people could take their paper money to banks and exchange it for gold coins. That limited the amount of paper money printed to the amount of gold held by the government. McKinley pledged to stick with gold. William Jennings Bryan, the Democratic candidate for president, wanted to expand the economy by backing the dollar with gold *and* silver.

On a stop in Colorado, Roosevelt visited a silver mining town where voters greatly favored the two metal standard. TR met with strong opposition. People threw rocks. Roosevelt was hit in the chest with a six-foot-long stick. "But he was smiling and his eyes were dancing," someone who was there remembered later. "When it was all over, he exclaimed, 'This is magnificent. Why, it's the best time I've had since I started. I wouldn't have missed it for anything.'" He had what he called "a bully time" throughout the campaign.

On November 6, 1900, McKinley and Roosevelt won by 849,000 votes.

On March 4, 1901, Roosevelt was inaugurated as vice president. He took the oath of office and then spoke. "We belong to a young nation," he said. "East and West we look across two great oceans toward the larger world life in which, whether we will or not, we must take an ever-increasing share."

Roosevelt worked well with McKinley and his Cabinet. But he served as vice president for only six months and ten days. Then an assassin made Theodore Roosevelt, at forty-two, the youngest president in U.S. history.

Rough Rider Roosevelt, published in London's Punch *magazine just after he became President.*

7. President

"In this hour of deep and terrible bereavement," Roosevelt said before he took the oath of office as president, "I wish to state that it shall be my aim to continue absolutely unbroken the policy of President McKinley for the peace and prosperity of our beloved country." He asked members of McKinley's Cabinet to stay with him, and they did.

TR became president during a time of great change. People living in cities traveled on horse-drawn streetcars and electric-powered trolley cars. In the country, many still got around in ox carts. Americans owned just eight thousand cars in 1900, and they "shook and trembled, and clattered," according to one car

President Theodore Roosevelt, 1901.

owner of the era, and "spat oil, fire, smoke, and smell." They were play-things for the wealthy. By the end of the decade that would change. By 1910 there were almost five hundred thousand registered cars in the United States.

There were no airplanes in 1901. Orville and Wilbur Wright's first flight, less than one shaky minute in the air, wouldn't happen until December 1903.

Most households didn't have telephones. In a nation of seventy-six million people, there were just six hundred thousand telephones. Within ten years there would be ten times that many.

Most Americans were poor. Eighty percent had no savings and lived a day-to-day existence. In cities many lived in dingy tenement apartments with smelly outhouses as toilets. Because it was a lot of work to heat enough water on the stove to fill a tub, people bathed just once a week, usually in the kitchen or on the back porch. By 1910 plans for new houses almost always showed an indoor bathroom.

In 1900 lots of children played and worked in the streets peddling newspapers, matches, breads, and cakes. Garbage piled up in those city streets, attracting stray dogs, cats, mice, and rats. By the early 1900s people were becoming aware of the harmful effects of some bacteria and other invisible life-forms. Major efforts to clean up America's cities were begun.

In 1900 there was a great divide between the rich and poor. While some workers earned as little as six dollars a week, Andrew Carnegie, one of America's richest men, made about $23 million yearly.

Roosevelt was aware of all this, and insisted that every American be given a "square deal."

TR was a different kind of president. With his varied background, he seemed to represent the entire nation. He was born in

Andrew Carnegie (1835–1919).

the East, was the son of a Southern belle, and was a champion of the rugged lifestyle of the West.

In 1908 a *New York Times* reporter spent an entire week with Roosevelt. He wrote in the newspaper's "Sunday Magazine" that before he began working on the article, he never thought Roosevelt was "particularly admirable," but after a week with the president, his opinion changed.

He wrote that Roosevelt was constantly moving, and when TR spoke, his entire body did the talking. "Remember that Mr. Roosevelt never speaks a word in the ordinary conversational tone. He utters everything with immense emphasis. His face energized, from the base of the neck to the roots of the hair." But "the President is a joker. He is always looking for fun—and always finding it." And then when he breaks into "a roar of laughter . . . the fun engulfs his whole face: his eyes close, and speech expires in a silent gasp of joy."

In his office, on a typical morning, the president met with some two hundred government officials and private citizens. He walked from one to the next, shook each person's hand, and then listened. Sometimes he listened for less than a minute, and sometimes for as long as an hour. He gave his answer to the issue raised, and moved on. The questions varied greatly, but he was able to focus on them all. He was obsessed with learning all the relevant facts, and then, when he made a decision, he couldn't be talked out of it. He was strong-willed, and according to the *Times* reporter, "He maintains his right to have his way—on the ground that his way is right."

The article was unsigned. "The testimony is that of one whose name, of course, is of not the slightest

Roosevelt talking, adapted from a 1910 German cartoon.

consequence," the reporter wrote of himself. Then he wrote his evaluation of the president.

"He is, first of all, a physical marvel. He radiates energy as the sun radiates light and heat, and he does it apparently without losing a particle of his own energy. It is not merely remarkable, it is a simple miracle, that this man can keep up day after day."

That TR could talk!

The writer Rudyard Kipling witnessed him discussing men, politics, and books. "I curled up on the seat opposite," Kipling said, "and listened . . . until the universe seemed to be spinning and Theodore was the spinner."

TR's sister Corinne visited often, especially at diplomatic dinners, and stood nearby as he welcomed the long line of guests. "Almost always," she later remembered, "he would have some special word for each . . . almost every person who passed him would have that extraordinary sense that he or she was personally recognized."

His sister wrote that some people mistook his strong convictions "for an egotistical inability to look at it any other way. When he was convinced that his attitude was correct . . . nothing could swerve him; but when, as was often the case, it was not a question of conviction, but of advisability, he was the most open minded of men."

Another frequent White House visitor was his former tutor Dr. Cutler. TR was a voracious reader, and sometime during each visit he asked, "What have you been reading?" Cutler answered, and time after time, his former student had already read the book. Cutler was determined to get ahead of Roosevelt, so before a visit to the White House he bought a two-volume nonfiction title that had just been published. He read the first two hundred pages on the train ride from New York to Washington. But TR was ahead of him. When Cutler told him what he had been reading, the president said, "Wait till you get to page 455 of volume two; that is where the work shines."

"The door of the White House," Roosevelt said soon after he

took office, "shall swing open as easily for the poor as for the rich." In 1901 that policy got him into trouble.

On October 1, 1901, just a few weeks after he became president, he met with Dr. Booker T. Washington, a former slave who was now the head of the Tuskegee Institute in Alabama, a vocational school for African Americans. Roosevelt consulted with Washington on finding qualified black and white Southerners to fill government positions.

On October 7 Roosevelt appointed an Alabama man, Thomas Goode Jones, to be a U.S. district judge. TR was a Republican and Jones was a Democrat, but according to Washington he was the best man for the job, and that was what Roosevelt wanted.

Dr. Booker T. Washington (1856–1915).

On October 16 Roosevelt invited Washington to have dinner with him in the White House. This was the first time any president made such an invitation to an African American. Many Southern whites were appalled. They accused TR of planning to have African Americans rule the South.

In later years Washington spoke not of the food that night, but of the others at the table. He said, "I dined with the president and members of his family." These included President and Mrs. Roosevelt, their children Kermit, Ethel, Archie, and Quentin, and TR's Colorado hunting friend Philip Stewart.

According to one Tennessee newspaper, the dinner was a "damnable outrage." Another Tennessee newspaper declared, "President Roosevelt has committed a blunder that is worse than a crime."

The dinner convinced blacks that they had a friend in the White House. In some ways they did. Roosevelt continued to seek advice from Washington. He invited other African Americans to formal receptions. But not to dinner. He did not want to lose whatever white support he still had in the South.

By 1903 Washington was a controversial figure even in the African-American community. Dr. W.E.B. Du Bois, another great black leader, the first to be awarded a doctorate from Harvard University, was more militant and disagreed with Washington's philosophy. Du Bois believed college and professional education, not vocational training, were the surest paths to equality.

Roosevelt's dinner with Washington made it appear that he was a true supporter of equality for all races. But he did not support easier access for blacks to the voting booth. He did not appoint a great number of blacks to federal jobs. And in 1906 he seemed to cross the line and support unfair treatment of blacks.

In what became known as the Brownsville Affair, it was reported that a handful of African-American soldiers, apparently upset at prejudicial treatment by the locals, snuck out of camp one night. They shot up the town, killing one white and wounding another. Then they returned to camp unnoticed. According to some people, these were false charges and the evidence had all been planted. When no one would admit to the shooting, and no one would turn in fellow soldiers, Roosevelt ordered that all three companies of blacks stationed there, one hundred sixty-seven soldiers, be given dishonorable discharges. They all lost their pensions, including six men who had received Medals of Honor.

Dr. Washington protested. Secretary of War William Howard Taft asked to reopen the case. But the president refused.

Theodore Roosevelt was the youngest president in our nation's history and he had young children. When he first became president, Alice was seventeen. Theodore Jr. was fourteen; Kermit was almost twelve; Ethel was ten; Archibald was seven; and Quentin was not yet four years old.

"All children should have just as good a time as they possibly

President Roosevelt and his family in 1901, from left to right: Quentin, the President, Theodore, Jr., Archibald, Alice Lee, Kermit, Mrs. Roosevelt, and Ethel.

can," TR wrote before he became president. Beginning in September 1901 he could have added, "even in the White House."

TR's children "took delight in roller skating, bike-riding, and walking on stilts" in the White House, according to Irwin Hood Hoover, the chief usher.

"Nothing," according to friend William Thayer, "interfered with the seclusion of the family breakfast. There were no guests, only Mrs. Roosevelt and the children." The meal "was quiet, private, uninterrupted. Then each member of the family would go about his or her work, for idleness had no place with them."

Alice was TR's eldest child, his daughter from his first marriage. She was a beautiful but rebellious young woman. There was almost no telling what she might do. She gambled, smoked cigarettes, stayed out late partying, and often had a live garter snake in the pocket of her dress. On an official U.S. mission cruise to Asia, she jumped fully clothed into the ship's pool. "I can be president of the United States," TR said, "or I can attend to Alice. I cannot possibly do both."

It wasn't always easy being a Roosevelt. "Poor TR Jr.," Alice said of her half brother, because whenever he did something, "someone has something to say because he doesn't do it as his father would." Rev. Iglehart wrote of TR Jr., "In his facial expressions, his movements, his warm handshake, his polite demeanor and mental virility he reminds one very much of his father."

TR's third child, his son Kermit, "looks so much like his father," Rev. Iglehart wrote, "as to soften my heart." Kermit was a big-game hunter, and on the African safari with his father, in a terribly frightening moment, he was stalking a lion when a leopard attacked. At the very last moment, Kermit shot the leopard.

TR's daughter Ethel was, according to Iglehart, "the apple of her father's eye, his companion as a romping girl and his help as a mature woman." One fortunate errand for her father led to her marriage.

TR had heard that a neighborhood family was too poor to pay for the foot surgery their son needed. He sent Ethel to meet the family and tell them to take the boy to Roosevelt Hospital, and that TR would pay the bill. The operation was a complete success, and Ethel met the boy's surgeon, Dr. Richard Derby.

"It was the most natural thing in the world for Miss Ethel Carow Roosevelt and Dr. Richard Derby to fall in love," according to a newspaper report announcing their engagement, "because they are both in love with a good horse and ardently devoted to outdoor sports and exercise." The report described their relationship as "a romance of the saddle."

Ethel Roosevelt and Richard Derby married on April 4, 1913.

TR's fifth child, Archibald, according to Rev. Iglehart, like his father had "a bright eye, a strong grip, and a kindly spirit." He was playful. During the family's White House years, he slid down a banister into the middle of a formal diplomatic reception.

TR's youngest child, Quentin, "possessed evidences of the highest genius," according to Iglehart. He was often the target of reporters looking for inside information about his father, but they couldn't trap Quentin. "I see him occasionally," he once answered, "but I know nothing of his family life."

TR played wildly with his children in the White House. They raced through the halls and had pillow fights.

In January 1904 nine-year-old Archie entered the White House loaded with snowballs. He threw them at a doorman, but missed. Another doorman saw what was happening and escaped into the Cabinet room. Archie threw a snowball at a Secret Service agent and missed again. Then he went outside "to pelt the big policeman who stands all day in front of the Executive Mansion. . . . They soon had a good time, and the boy was himself made to feel the sting there is in a snowball well made and nicely thrown."

Once, while TR was meeting with a congressman, Archie brought a large king snake to show his father. It delighted the president but frightened the congressman.

When Archie was sick, his younger brother Quentin and the stable boy snuck a calico pony into the elevator and brought it upstairs to visit.

There were also uninvited animals in and around the White House. One time there were newspaper reports that the house was overrun with rats, and people sent TR traps. Someone sent him five cats.

TR was an avid naturalist and he took note of the wildlife just outside the White House. "A pair of red-headed woodpeckers," he recorded in his journal, "have nested for three years in the White House grounds." He wrote of mockingbirds, wood thrushes, robins, song sparrows, crows, orioles, scarlet tanagers, tufted titmice, cardinals, and catbirds all living nearby. "The hearty, wholesome songs of the robins," he wrote, "and the sweet homelike strains of the song sparrow are the first to be regularly heard in the grounds,

President Roosevelt on horseback, 1901.

and they lead the chorus." He saw rabbits and possums on the grounds. He had squirrels eating out of his hand.

Roosevelt was no less active than his children. He boxed, wrestled, and went horseback riding. In 1905 an accident forced him to give up boxing.

"I used to box with one of my aides," he said in a 1917 interview. "One day he cross-countered me and broke a blood vessel in my left eye. . . . I have never been able to see out of that eye since. I thought, as only one good eye was left me, I would not box any longer."

Until that interview, no one knew of the accident. Even Colonel Dan Moore, the aide who boxed with the president, didn't know.

"I give you my word I never knew I had blinded the Colonel in one eye until I read his statement in the paper a few days ago," Moore said in 1917. "When you put on gloves with President Roosevelt it was a case of fight all the way, and no man in the ring with him had a chance to keep track of particular blows. . . . The Colonel wanted plenty of action, and he usually got it. He had no use for a quitter or one who gave ground, and nobody but a man willing to fight all the time and all the way had a chance with him."

Moore wrote to Roosevelt to apologize for the injury.

TR's response was "There is nothing more to say about the matter." He hadn't spoken of it for twelve years, and probably had no intention of speaking of it again. That was his code, established as a child suffering from severe asthma, in the Maine woods, and in the Wild West. Roosevelt didn't complain of personal injury or discomfort, even as president.

Charles Lee was TR's chauffeur and coachman during most of his White House years and all the years that followed. "I was counted quite a driver of horses," Lee remembered in 1919, "for they used horses more than cars at that time. . . . Mr. Roosevelt was devoted to his horses; he was a splendid rider—sat to the saddle perfectly—had easy control of his horse and enjoyed riding, as a sport and exercise, amazingly." He and his wife liked to ride every morning. "He never seemed so happy as when he was with Mrs. Roosevelt, and never happier than when they went out together on these morning rides which lasted usually a couple of hours."

Whenever the Roosevelts could manage it, the family went back to their home in Oyster Bay. When the president arrived he was greeted by the family's four to five dogs, who barked and jumped on him. Then TR and his canine friends walked through his property to inspect the many shrubs and trees he had planted. They walked past the burial plots of his children's pets—guinea pigs, rabbits, and rats.

By the front of the house was a large wooden box with glass windows, a feeder for wild birds. Every morning when he was home, TR stopped by the box and fed the birds.

Often he was in Oyster Bay, Roosevelt often threw a picnic basket filled with food into a rowboat, evaded the Secret Service men who guarded him, and went off for a day just with his family. He swam with his boys and camped out with them. They fished and he did the cooking. When it got dark they gathered around the fire and told ghost stories. Other days, when the president wanted to be alone, he put on a work shirt, took an ax, found some hidden place in the woods, and chopped down trees.

"I have met Mr. Roosevelt coming in with his ax," journalist and friend Jacob Riis wrote in 1904. Riis was sure TR's opponents "would have a hard time resisting the swing of that strong and righteous arm."

TR did everything with gusto, including eating. "I eat too much," he told his son Kermit. And he ate too fast. He was described as "eating like a machine." He was known to eat a whole chicken at a meal, along with various side dishes and four glasses of milk. He drank lots of tea and coffee, and with each cup he took five to seven lumps of sugar. But he didn't drink alcohol.

Along with his odd eating habits, TR had another strange practice for a president. He knew it took just one bullet to kill even the most popular man. In his own lifetime, three presidents had been assassinated—Lincoln, Garfield, and McKinley. TR was not the type to depend on others for his protection. According to a 1912 report in the *New York Times*, "Colonel Roosevelt, during his seven and a half years as President, never went on the streets without a revolver in his pocket."

On one Western trip he stopped in St. Paul, Minnesota. Somehow his and Governor Samuel Van Sant's overcoats were switched. The next morning, after TR left town, Van Sant put his hand into what he thought was his coat pocket and found a new large-caliber gun. He looked at the label inside the garment and discovered that both the coat and the gun belonged to the president.

By 1904, according to the *Times*, "Roosevelt was getting portly and the strain on the waist line of his frock coats had a tendency to make his coat tails spread apart." At times this gave onlookers a glimpse of "the butt of a good-sized revolver."

Edith Roosevelt, the president's wife, had a very different personality than her husband. She was more of a homebody, more genteel. She belonged to a Long Island church sewing circle. There she and about twenty other women made clothes for disabled children. What she didn't finish in the circle, she brought back to the White House and finished there.

In 1904 Roosevelt was the Republican Party candidate for president. "Of course, I am excited about the election," he wrote to his sister Corinne in October, "but there really isn't much I can do about it, and I confine myself chiefly to the regular presidential work."

Corinne wrote much later, "The one great ambition of Theodore Roosevelt's life was to be chosen President on his own merits by the people of the United States. He longed for the seal of approval on the devoted service which he had rendered to his country."

His running mate was Senator Charles W. Fairbanks of Indiana. Fairbanks, like Roosevelt four years before, campaigned widely. He traveled more than twenty-five thousand miles to thirty-three states.

TR campaigned, too, and he had a style all his own.

One day he stood in Atlanta before a hostile crowd that shouted and jeered and wouldn't let him speak. The president was determined to be heard, so he jumped onto a table. The noise of him landing on the tabletop and the sight of him standing there startled his audience. They were quiet long enough for Roosevelt to get into his speech.

1904 Roosevelt-Fairbanks Campaign Poster.

In November 1904 Roosevelt and Fairbanks handily beat their Democratic opponents, Judge Alton B. Parker of New York and eighty-year-old former senator Henry G. Davis of West Virginia. On the night of his election, Roosevelt called the accepted two-term limit for presidents a "wise custom" and declared, "Under no circumstances will I be a candidate for and accept the nomination for another."

Inauguration Day, March 4, 1905, was dark, windy, and threatening rain. At about noon, Roosevelt walked out onto a platform erected on the east side of the Capitol. Despite the weather, thousands of people stood in the nearby plaza and in the streets. They saw TR stand straight, with his chest out, like a soldier, and rest his hand on an open Bible. "I, Theodore Roosevelt," he said, and took the oath of office.

After the inauguration there was a luncheon at the White House with friends from New York, the Maine woods, and the Dakotas. Then Roosevelt stood on a reviewing stand and saluted the huge parade of supporters including West Point and Navel Academy cadets, governors on horseback, cowboys waving lassos, and American Indians including Chief Joseph of the Nez Percé tribe. At the end of the day, the President had just one regret. He said, wistfully, "How I wished Father could have been here to see it too!"

Theodore Roosevelt on the way to his inauguration, March 4, 1905.

8. Trustbuster

Theodore Roosevelt pledged to "Give every man a fair chance." "Don't let any one harm him," he said, "and don't let him harm any one." That was a tough task in 1901. At the time, there was great danger that the nation would soon become a plutocracy— that the government would be controlled by a small group of wealthy people. Small companies were being taken over by larger ones, and monopolies were being formed. Roosevelt didn't let that happen.

At the time, traveling and shipping goods by rail was the only choice most people had. In November 1901, shortly after Roosevelt became president, the Great Northern, Northern Pacific, Chicago, Burlington, and Quincy railroads were merged to form a company called Northern Securities, a railroad monopoly in the northwestern section of the country. Without competition, this newly formed trust could charge unfairly high prices. Roosevelt ordered that the Jus-

Roosevelt beats the beef trust.

tice Department sue the company. In 1904 the case came before the Supreme Court and the railroad trust was broken.

Roosevelt successfully went after the "Beef Trust," the Standard Oil Company, and the American Tobacco Company. He sued more than forty monopolies and broke many of them.

He became known as "the Trustbuster."

Early in Roosevelt's presidency, there were rumors of corruption in the U.S. Post Office. He was told to handle the situation quietly, to protect the reputation of his political party. But there was nothing quiet about Roosevelt. He ordered an investigation and that anyone guilty of fraud be fired.

A huge sugar importing company had cheated the government out of at least $2 million dollars in import taxes. In these and other cases, the president was relentless. He would not let the super-rich twist and break the law.

In the fall of 1902, in Pennsylvania, there was a coal miners strike. The workers wanted a shorter day, higher wages, and their union to be recognized as the representative of all the miners. Coal fueled the nation's furnaces, factories, and railroads. Without coal, "A calamity threatened," according to the president's friend Thayer, "quite as terrible as the invasion of an enemy's army."

Roosevelt summoned representatives of both sides to the White House. He was in a wheelchair when they arrived, the result of an accident. The horse-drawn carriage he was in had been hit by a trolly. The Secret Service man with TR was killed. The president was more fortunate: he was thrown forty feet from the carriage but suffered only a broken leg.

At the meeting George F. Baer, who represented the mine owners, called John Mitchell, the union leader of the strike, a "criminal." Baer refused to speak directly to Mitchell. Roosevelt was furious. "If it wasn't for the high office I hold," he said, "I would have taken him by the seat of the breeches and the nape of the neck and chucked him out of that window."

"Some men," Mitchell said, "who own the mines think they own the men, too; and some men who work in the mines think they own them. Both are wrong."

Roosevelt was ready to send in federal troops to work the mines. To stop that from happening, the mine owners allowed a commission to arbitrate the dispute, and the miners went back to work.

In the final agreement the miners' workday was shortened to nine hours and they got more pay, but their union was still not recognized.

The coal strike was stressful for TR. After he settled it he went on a bear hunt in Mississippi, but that was stressful, too. There were no bears. At last an old black bear wandered into the camp and killed one of the dogs in the president's party. The bear was caught and tied to a tree and Roosevelt was called to kill it, but he refused. He wouldn't shoot a defenseless animal. The incident was reported and the American people loved it. A New York toy shop owner made a toy bear to honor Roosevelt's sportsmanlike behavior, and

"PROTECT AND PRESERVE THE REMAINING FORESTS UPON PUBLIC LANDS FROM DEVASTATION AND DESTRUCTION, WHICH HAVE BEEN THE FATE OF THOSE IN FOREST SECTIONS OF THE COUNTRY."

is said to have asked that he be allowed to name the toy after TR. "I don't think my name will mean much to the bear business," was the rumored reply, "but you're welcome to use it." And so the "teddy bear" was born.

The Trustbuster President could also be called the Conservation President. He created a national policy on the preservation of the country's natural resources—the land, forests, and water on the earth and the minerals within it. He saved for future generations Arizona's Grand Canyon and Petrified Forest, New York's Niagara Falls, Oregon's Crater Lake, and other natural wonders. He established five new national parks including South Dakota's Wind Cave and Colorado's Mesa Verde. In 1906 he urged the passage of the National Monuments Act, which saved California's Muir Woods and many other great sites. He created fifty-one wildlife sanctuaries, one hundred fifty national forests, and four game preserves. He added more than two hundred million acres to the land under government protection.

There were other great challenges for TR. At the beginning of the twentieth century popular ten-cent magazines published many reports on the horrors of city living, child labor, racial bigotry, and political corruption. Best-selling books such as Sinclair Lewis's *The Jungle,* which detailed health horrors in the meatpacking industry, were calls to action and Roosevelt responded. He championed better working conditions for women and children and better living conditions for everyone.

Women became ever more active, especially in their attacks on saloons and drinking. By 1900 there were ten thousand local branches of the Women's Christian Temperance Union. They saw alcohol as one cause of wife and child abuse and of poverty. They campaigned for women's rights, especially the right to vote, and Roosevelt supported that.

TR also had personal domestic triumphs.

"The quality of sharing," Corinne wrote of her brother Theodore, "was one of his most marked attributes, never showed more unselfishly than in times of sorrow." She was writing about the shared loss of their brother Elliot.

Elliot Roosevelt was mentally unstable. He was an alcoholic. In August 1894 he went on a drunken carriage ride, crashed, injured his head, and drank some more. Then he attempted suicide, had an epileptic seizure, and died. He was just thirty-four years old. His wife, Anna, had died two years before of diphtheria. Their daughter, Eleanor, was raised by relatives.

On December 1, 1904, Eleanor's engagement to marry Franklin Delano Roosevelt, a distant cousin, was announced.

"We are greatly rejoiced over the good news," Eleanor's uncle Theodore wrote to the groom-to-be. "I am as fond of Eleanor as if she were my daughter, and I like you, and trust you, and believe in you. No other success in life—not the Presidency or anything else—begins to compare with the joy and happiness that come in and from the love of the true man and the true woman."

Like TR, Franklin Roosevelt would be an assistant secretary of the Navy, governor of New York, and president of the United States. He would be elected to four consecutive terms as president, beginning in 1932.

Edith Roosevelt offered to have the wedding in the White House. "Your uncle and I," she wrote, "would like to have your

Eleanor Roosevelt (1884–1962).

President Franklin Delano Roosevelt (1882–1945).

marriage under his roof and make all the arrangements for it." But Eleanor kept to her plans to have the wedding in New York City, at the home of her cousins Susie and Henry Parish.

The wedding was on March 17, 1905. It was a busy day for the president. He reviewed the city's Saint Patrick's Day parade, made a couple of speeches, and walked his niece down the aisle in place of his deceased brother. When the minister asked, "Who giveth this woman in marriage?" it was Theodore who answered rather loudly, "I do."

Less than one year later, on February 17, 1906, there was another Roosevelt wedding. This time it was in the White House. TR's daughter Alice married Congressman Nicholas Longworth of Ohio. They were married in the East Room. According to a newspaper report, "It was a glorious day, and all through the big crowd which lined the streets and pressed eager faces against the White House palings people were quoting old proverbs and predicting all kinds of happiness for the bride." Of the bride the newspaper reported, "She was as happy a bride as ever was married." She wore a white satin gown trimmed with lace, and long white gloves. And of the groom, who was fourteen years older than Alice, it reported, "He was one broad beam of sunshine from that much-advertised bald head to his feet." He wore a "frock coat with black trousers" and "pearl-gray gloves." Alice cut the wedding cake with a sword she borrowed from one of the military men. Among the guests were foreign diplomats, the vice president, members of the Cabinet, the Ohio congressional delegation, Supreme Court justices, and Mrs. Nellie Grant Sartoris, the daughter of President Grant. In 1874 Sartoris had been married in the same room.

It wasn't a happy marriage. In the 1912 presidential campaign, Longworth supported President Taft instead of his father-in-law, TR, and Alice did not forgive him for that. Longworth loved whisky and other women. Alice was also unfaithful. In 1925 Alice gave birth to Paulina, but the baby's father was not her husband. It was Senator William Borah of Idaho.

President Theodore Roosevelt, 1903.

9. The Big Stick

Theodore Roosevelt said it was his policy to "speak softly and carry a big stick." Many people feared he wasn't content to simply *carry* the stick. They worried that he would be a war-thirsty president.

People who knew him worried, too. In 1885 his college friend Charles Washburn had seen him in Chicago with a rifle on his shoulder. He was on his way to the Dakota Territory. "I urged him to give up his frontier life," Washburn said, "but he is charmed with it and wants to be killing something all the time."

In December 1895 TR had told his friend Massachusetts Senator Henry Cabot Lodge, "This country needs a war." Another of his friends, President Eliot of Harvard, was appalled by what he called "this chip-on-the-shoulder attitude." He likened it to the manner of a "ruffian and a bully."

"The victories of peace are great," TR said two years later. "The victories of war are greater."

On December 3, 1901, Roosevelt delivered his first message to Congress. He had been president for less than three months. It was a somewhat peace-loving message. Perhaps the presidency had softened him.

"This nation most earnestly desires sincere and cordial friendship with all others," he said. "More and more, the civilized peoples are realizing the wicked folly of war."

But he also knew that a strong Army and Navy would be his "big stick."

As a former assistant secretary of the Navy, he had a special interest in that branch of service. "The work of upbuilding the Navy must be steadily continued," he said in the same speech. "It is not possible to improvise a navy after war breaks out."

On December 2, 1902, he delivered his second message. He spoke of the Army, which, he said, "is very small for the size of the nation." He wanted soldiers to get added training. "The marksmanship of the men must receive special attention. . . . In battle the only shots that count are the shots that hit." Of the Navy he said, "We need a thousand additional officers in order to properly man the ships now provided for and under construction. . . . There seems not the slightest chance of trouble with a foreign power. We must earnestly hope that this state of things may continue; and the way to insure its continuance is to provide for a thoroughly efficient navy."

He also spoke of a canal through the isthmus connecting North and South America. The canal would be a boon to business because to get from one coast of the country to the other, ships would no longer have to travel around the southern tip of South America. Moving goods between the east and west coasts would be cheaper. It would also help the military, since Navy ships could more quickly move between the Atlantic and Pacific oceans. The proposed canal was to cut through Panama, a region of Colombia, but the leaders of that country refused to agree to the terms proposed by the U.S.

Roosevelt wasn't the first one to talk of a canal. In the mid-1500s, King Charles V had searched for a shortcut from his country, Spain, to its colony Peru on the western coast of South America.

In 1881 a French company began work on a canal, but accidents and disease, mostly malaria and yellow fever, cost more than twenty thousand lives, and in 1893 it gave up. In 1904 the United States paid the French $40 million for whatever rights and equipment they still had in Panama.

Roosevelt gets the Panama Canal built.

Others talked about building a canal. But Roosevelt got it done.

In November 1903 a revolution broke out in Colombia; it had been quietly encouraged by President Roosevelt. Panama's rebels wanted to separate their section from the rest of the country. As soon as TR heard of the revolt, he recognized the new government of Panama, which controlled the area of the proposed canal. Two weeks later that new government signed a treaty granting the U.S. the right to build the canal.

The canal was completed in 1914. That year about one thousand ships passed through it. Today about fifteen thousand go through each year.

During TR's first year as president, there was other trouble south of the U.S. border. The government of Venezuela owed several million dollars to German and British banks. When it didn't pay, the governments of both Germany and England cut off diplomatic relations with the country. Their warships sailed to the coast of Venezuela and fired on the country's ships and ports. They threatened to seize Venezuelan property.

President Roosevelt summoned the German ambassador to the White House. TR told him that unless Germany was willing to settle the dispute peaceably, he would send U.S. warships to the area to defend Venezuela. They agreed to bring the issue to the Permanent Court of Arbitration in The Hague, Holland, which set a payment plan for the debt.

TR had waved his "big stick" and got results.

In 1896 gold was discovered in the Klondike, in northwestern Canada very close to the Alaskan border. This led to a border dispute. In 1903 it was settled by arbitration, mostly favoring the U.S. Of course this pleased TR. He said the settlement showed "the fairness and good-will with which two friendly nations can approach and determine issues."

In 1904, near the end of Roosevelt's first term in office, there was an international crisis in Morocco. An American who lived there,

Ion Perdicaris, and his stepson were kidnapped by Mulai Ahmed er Raisuli, a tribal leader. Some Moroccan people considered Raisuli to be a hero, a sort of "Robin Hood." Others saw him as a brutal bandit. Roosevelt sent seven U.S. warships to the area, along with this message: "Perdicaris alive or Raisuli dead." A month later the two men were released unharmed, though probably before TR's warning reached Raisuli.

Also in 1904, there was war in the East between Japan and Russia. Japan had significant victories, but the fighting had weakened its forces. Russia was a vast country with a huge population and could surely have fought on, but it had its own internal troubles and was eager to end the war.

TR contacted Czar Nicholas II of Russia and sent an official note to Emperor Meiji of Japan, urging them to consider making peace. In August 1905 representatives from both countries met with Roosevelt in Portsmouth, New Hampshire. During the talks, Roosevelt wrote in a letter, what he needed to do was "be polite and sympathetic in explaining for the hundredth time something perfectly obvious." But what he wanted to do, he said, was "give utterance to rage and jump up and knock their heads together." His patience paid off. On September 5, 1905, the delegates signed a treaty, and Roosevelt, whose friends had worried he would be a war-thirsty president, was declared the great peacemaker. The next year he was awarded the Nobel Peace Prize.

In 1906 Roosevelt stepped in again in another Japanese matter. The San Francisco Board of Education had ordered the transfer of Japanese, Chinese, and Korean children from the city's regular public schools to the Oriental Public School. There was outrage here and in Japan. There was even talk in Japan of declaring war on the United States. Roosevelt called this act of segregation a "wicked absurdity" and convinced the members of the board to revoke the order. In return, he worked out an agreement with Japan to limit the number of its citizens emigrating to the United States.

In September 1906 there was trouble again in Cuba, the beginnings of a revolution brought on by a suspected rigged election. TR sent in several thousand sailors and soldiers to restore order and to protect U.S. investments. In November 1908 new elections supervised by the U.S. military were held, a stable Cuban government took over, and in February 1909 American forces left the island.

What sort of president was Theodore Roosevelt?

"He can lead an army in the teeth of battle and never flinch," Frank A. Munsey of *Munsey's Magazine* wrote in 1904. "With equal courage he can say, and say with terrible emphasis 'Yes,' or 'No!' He dares to do right as he understands the right, and he dares to defy wrong as he sees the wrong."

"I have had a corking time," Roosevelt said when he left the White House. He didn't believe any president had had as good a time in office as he had. He was probably right.

10. African Safari and Welcome Home

After his election in 1904, Roosevelt had said he would not be a candidate for president in 1908. He kept his word. Instead, he urged the Republican Party to choose William Howard Taft of Ohio, at the time his good friend and secretary of war.

Taft was an uneasy politician.

"Poor old boy!" Roosevelt wrote to him. "Of course you are not enjoying the campaign. I wish you had some of my bad temper!"

"Hit them hard, old man!" Roosevelt advised later, and added, "Let the audience see you smile."

People wrote letters to Roosevelt complaining that Taft played golf, a rich man's sport. "It would seem incredible that anyone would care one way or the other," TR wrote to a friend. "It is just like my tennis; I never let any friends advertise my tennis, and never let a photograph of me in tennis costume appear."

Roosevelt backs the nomination of William Howard Taft for president.

President William Howard Taft (1857–1930).

Despite his troubles campaigning, on November 3 Taft was elected with well over one million more votes than his Democratic opponent, William Jennings Bryan. But that easy victory was a large drop-off from Roosevelt's margin of more than two and a half million in 1904.

Thursday, March 4, 1909, the day of the inauguration, the outgoing and incoming presidents had breakfast together. Outside was a treacherous snowstorm, and TR joked, "I knew there would be a blizzard clear up to the minute I went out of office."

Immediately after the ceremony the Roosevelts left Washington. Three weeks later TR and his son Kermit were on their way to eastern and central Africa to hunt. TR planned to send animals and plants to the Smithsonian Institution in Washington. "Kermit and I kept about a dozen trophies for ourselves," TR later said. "Otherwise we shot

Roosevelt and Taft on their way to the Capitol for President Taft's inauguration, March 4, 1909.

nothing that was not used either as a museum specimen or for meat—usually for both purposes."

TR would display his trophies—the stuffed animals or animal heads—in his home.

The Roosevelts didn't travel alone. R. J. Cuninghame, a well-known African hunter, headed the expedition. Also along were a famous big-game hunter named Selous and a lecturer on exotic travel named Newman, a few naturalists, and about four hundred Africans who set up the tents, took care of the horses, and carried the supplies. In addition there were fifteen soldiers along to protect the former president.

*"The Frightened Animals," a New York newspaper cartoon
of the reaction to Roosevelt's planned safari.*

"I have taken many well-known people on hunting trips," Cuning-hame later said, "but I have never found any other so easy to get along with and I have never known any other man who by his character made every man in his service as anxious to do the best possible for him."

Roosevelt was a good shot, according to Cuninghame. "You could always rely on his hitting his animal and, if he did not put the shot in the right place, of hitting him again and again until he dropped him."

TR had many adventures, including an encounter with an angry hippopotamus. The hunters found it in shallow water at the edge of a lake. TR, Kermit, and Cuninghame got into a small boat and rowed toward the animal. It was facing the other way and didn't see them approach. When they were close, Roosevelt lifted his rifle and shot the hippo in its shoulder. The animal turned, opened its huge mouth, and rushed at the hunters. Kermit took numerous photographs as his father shot again and again at the charging hippo. Just before the huge animal reached the boat, one of TR's shots stopped it.

He had another "very near squeak," according to Cuninghame. "He was determined to get an elephant and a tusker at that. I told him what that meant and how much risk there was, but he said he was willing to face it. That was the Colonel all over. Tell him the risks and he would size them up quietly. If he decided they were worthwhile that was all there was to it."

Cuninghame described the "near squeak."

"Well, we found an elephant in a forest on Kenia Mountain. . . . I pointed it out to the Colonel and he fired with complete coolness and got the elephant in the ear and dropped him. . . . I never saw a man so boyishly jubilant, waving his hat and dancing about. . . . But half an hour later, when we were back in camp and the elephant had been handed over to the scientists, he sat down in a chair and started to read Balzac."

"The Colonel has been called a game butcher," Cuninghame said. "It was absolutely false. He went out with the definite purpose of

Roosevelt on his African safari, 1910.

getting a collection of East African fauna for American natural history museums and he kept that always in view. . . . That is the reason why he shot females. The ordinary sportsman, of course, never kills females, but the Colonel's idea was to get complete family groups of animals, many species of which will be extinct in a few years."

Roosevelt claimed to love animals. In 1907 he told his friend Jack Willis, who was in the business of killing animals for the skins, that what he was doing was "not just wrong; it is cowardly and contemptible and wicked." And yet TR was fascinated with "the kill" and seemed indifferent at times to animal and even human suffering. "Two days ago," he wrote from this trip to his friend Robert Bacon, "I saw one of the finest sights anyone can see: the Nandi warriors killed a lion with their spears, two of them (the warriors) being mauled."

Speaking through Europe, cartoon in a German newspaper.

On the safari, Theodore and Kermit killed more than five hundred wild animals including monkeys, hyenas, gazelles, impalas, giraffes, rhinoceroses, hippopotamuses, elephants, zebras, lions, pythons, and one crocodile. The Roosevelts and the other hunters also killed birds, fish, and various reptiles, and collected thousands of plants, and sent them all to the Smithsonian.

In the late fall, after about eight months away, TR wrote in a letter to his wife, "Oh, sweetest of all sweet girls, last night I dreamed that I was with you. . . . Darling I love you so. . . . How very happy we have been for these last twenty-three years."

In March 1910 they were reunited. Mrs. Roosevelt and their daughter Ethel met TR and Kermit in Khartoum, Sudan. They traveled together to Cairo, Egypt, and from there they went on to Europe.

In Italy Roosevelt met with the king, Vittorio Emanuelle III. The two men had a macabre connection. The king had ascended to the throne in 1900 when his father, King Umberto I, was shot by Gaetano Bresci. In 1901 Roosevelt had become president when Leon Czolgosz shot William McKinley.

The Roosevelts traveled to France, Belgium, Holland, Denmark, and Norway. In Vienna Roosevelt met with Emperor Franz Joseph of Austria. In Germany he met with Kaiser Wilhelm II, who called him "my friend Roosevelt . . . the most distinguished American citizen." TR and the kaiser sat on horses and reviewed

Roosevelt travels through Europe, cartoon in the Boston Herald.

thousands of German troops, perhaps some of the same soldiers the Americans would fight in 1917 and 1918 when the U.S. joined the Allies in the First World War.

At the end of the day TR was asked how he felt. "Oh, bully, by George!" he replied. "And what a corking five hours in the saddle, too."

From there he went to England, where on May 20 he attended the funeral of King Edward VII as the official representative of the United States. Also there were more than seventy members of the world's royalty—kings, queens, dukes, duchesses, princes, princesses, tsars, and tsarinas. It was the last time so many would be together. In the coming war many of them would lose their thrones.

While he was there a British weekly described Roosevelt as "red-blooded, warm-hearted, reckless and wise. . . . Mr. Roosevelt does honor to a country where he is beyond comparison the most outstanding man, and of which, to all appearances, he might be, if he chose, President for life."

On June 18, 1910, Roosevelt returned to New York to a hero's welcome. During the harbor parade boats of all sizes escorted his ship, the *Kaiserin Auguste Victoria*. During the street parade an estimated one million people lined New York's Broadway and Fifth Avenue for a stretch of five miles. They cheered, whistled, and waved to their hero. Among them was a group of Rough Riders and other veterans of the Spanish-American War. TR's response to the welcome was: "Bully."

"He himself was the same Roosevelt," according to the *New York Times*' report of his return, "stout and tanned, explosive in utterance, emphatic, resourceful, and untiring. . . . One could see that he enjoyed every moment of the triumphal progress through his native city."

TR stood on the bridge of the *Kaiserin Auguste Victoria* as it sailed into New York Harbor. A great yacht pulled alongside and a young woman waved a pennant. According to the *Times*' report, "The Colonel waved his silk hat back and beamed and chuckled and smiled. Just then a clumsy scow pulled up on the opposite side . . . women were waving aprons wherever there was standing room. Roosevelt caught a glimpse of the new welcomers, quickly crossed to the other side of the bridge, and soon was bending far over, waving his hat and shouting, 'Fine! Fine! Oh, it's simply great!' "

After he got off the boat, he shook the hands of hundreds of well-wishers. "I'm so glad to see you," he told everyone. "But it wasn't said the way it looks in type," according to the newspaper's report. "The 'so' went off like a firecracker. The smile backed it up in a radiation of energy, and the hearty grip of the hand that came down upon its respondent with a bang emphasized again the exact meaning of the words."

After his New York City welcome, TR went home by railroad. He waved to the many people who waited at the stops and crossings along the way. Once home he was greeted by his neighbors.

TR had a great memory for faces and names. According to his friend Rev. Iglehart, "Colonel Roosevelt knew nearly every person in Oyster Bay." To prove it, Iglehart wrote about someone TR met at his Long Island homecoming.

"About seventeen years before the famous African hunting trip the Colonel was having some repairs made at Sagamore Hill." TR told one of the men he didn't like the way he was doing his work. "The response was short and sharp, 'I take my orders from the boss.' Roosevelt, therefore, spoke with the contractor and the work was soon changed." In 1910, on TR's return home, "on the long line among others, was the before-mentioned mechanic. He shook hands with the Colonel, received a few appropriate words, and passed on. He had gone, however, but a few steps, when Roosevelt reached after him, pulled him back and demanded with his hearty chuckle, 'Say, so you still take your orders from the boss?' "

TR was greatly pleased with the welcome, but realistic. The next day he told his sister Corinne, *"That type* of crowd, feeling *that* kind of way, means that within a very short time they will be throwing rotten eggs at me."

T.R. returns home, 1910.

Roosevelt riding a moose just before attending the "Bull Moose" convention, 1912.

11. Bull Moose

"I have thoroughly enjoyed myself," Roosevelt said upon his return. But he added, "I am more glad than I can say to get home, to be back in my own country, back among people I love." He went right to work to tell the American people his story. He wrote his autobiography, which was published in installments in *The Outlook*, a weekly magazine.

TR had resolved to stay out of politics, but clearly that was against his nature.

In 1908 he had supported Taft for president. By 1910 he and many other Republicans were disappointed in Taft, whose policies were too pro-business and did too little to support the average citizen. Taft allowed some protective tariffs to rise, leading to higher prices. He fired Gifford Pinchot, the chief of forestry services and a leader in the effort to conserve the nation's natural resources.

Many complained that Taft was too much of a compromiser and not enough of a leader. He was unassertive. His speaking and writing skills were poor. Perhaps Taft's greatest failing was that he wasn't Theodore Roosevelt.

Roosevelt refused to visit with President Taft in the White House. Taft wrote to TR that he had been conscientiously trying to carry out his polices, but admitted, "my method of doing so has not worked smoothly." Roosevelt's response was that he would keep his mind open as he kept his mouth shut.

By 1912 many Republicans were determined to leave the party if Taft was renominated. They wanted Roosevelt.

Taft called his detractors "neurotics." Roosevelt called Taft's supporters "men of cold heart and narrow mind." He described Taft's presidency as one of "dull timidity and dull inaction." Roosevelt and Taft had once been close friends. They were now political enemies.

Seven Republican governors of Western states visited Roosevelt in Oyster Bay to urge him to run for the Republican nomination. On February 24, 1912, he declared he would run. "The fight is on," he said.

During the campaign for delegates, Roosevelt and Taft met by chance in an Ohio train yard. According to Taft, "vanity and egotism" colored TR's talk. It was "I, I, I." Taft pointed out that neither Washington nor Jefferson had a third term. "Ask him," Taft said, "if he's going to have a third term, why not a fourth term, and why not for life."

Roosevelt won most of the delegates in the twelve states that held primaries. The people obviously wanted him. However, most of the delegates in the thirty-six states that did not hold primaries were for Taft, who the party bosses wanted.

Beginning on Tuesday, June 18, 1912, the Republican National Committee met in Chicago. It was a raucous convention with shouting and fistfights. It took until Saturday to have the 1,078 delegates approved and officially seated. That night President Taft won the Republican nomination with 561 votes.

Roosevelt was no longer there. When it became clear to him that he would not be nominated, he had bolted from the convention.

The people who left with Roosevelt spent the next few weeks organizing the Progressive Party, nicknamed the "Bull Moose Party" from TR's reply to someone at a rally who asked how he felt. He responded, "Like a bull moose." But it wasn't just his party. There were Progressive candidates for Senate and House seats and for all sorts of local posts.

Roosevelt on a tour through New Jersey before the Progressive Party convention in 1912.

Beginning on June 25, the Democratic National Convention was held in Baltimore. The first vote was taken on Saturday morning, but it wasn't until the forty-sixth ballot on Tuesday that Governor Woodrow Wilson of New Jersey was nominated. Governor Thomas R. Marshall of Indiana was chosen as his vice presidential running mate.

Roosevelt and Wilson stood for many of the same principles. Wilson's nomination was bad news for Roosevelt.

"Baltimore unmakes him," a *New York Times* editorial declared. "The Republican bolting adventure is now stripped of every shred of justifying principle. There remains only vindictive passion against President Taft and the determination to make sure of his defeat."

President Woodrow Wilson (1856–1924).

On August 6, in the same hall as the Republican convention seven weeks earlier, with flags and other decorations left from that convention, the newly formed Progressive Party met. At times it seemed more a religious meeting than a political one. Delegates loudly sang hymns including "Onward, Christian Soldiers." The new party proposed lots of reforms including lower tariffs, granting women the right to vote, outlawing child labor, pure-food laws, old-age and unemployment insurance, a minimum wage for women, income and inheritance taxes, and limiting the work day to eight hours.

In the early afternoon Roosevelt stood before the convention to give the keynote address. The thousands of delegates cheered and waved banners. TR looked toward his wife. He took off his hat and waved it at her, and many of the delegates took off their hats and waved them at Mrs. Roosevelt. Then the California delegation took the golden teddy bear they had brought and set it on the podium.

At last, after almost one hour of hoopla, Roosevelt gave his speech.

"I hope we shall win," he said, "and I believe that if we can wake the people to what the fight really means we shall win. But win or lose, we shall not falter.... Our cause is based on the eternal principles of righteousness; and even though we who now lead may for the time fail, in the end the cause itself shall triumph.... We stand at Armageddon," he said at the end of his speech, "and we battle for the Lord."

Roosevelt was the Progressive Party's candidate for president. Governor Hiram W. Johnson of California was the nominee for vice president.

The famous social worker and women's-rights advocate Jane Addams made a seconding speech. It was the first time a woman had so prominent a role at such a convention. In 1931 she would be awarded a Nobel Peace Prize for her work with the poor.

"It is idle now to argue whether women can play their part in politics," TR wrote Addams a few days later in a thank-you note, "because in this convention we saw the accomplished fact, and moreover, the women who have actively participated in this work of launching the new party represent all that we are most proud."

Roosevelt and other members of the party were mostly realistic about their chance of winning in November. In accepting the nomination, TR's running mate, Governor Johnson, told the convention, "I would rather go down to defeat with Theodore Roosevelt than to victory with any other presidential candidate."

Jane Addams (1860–1935).

It was a nasty campaign. TR was denounced in editorials in both pro-Democratic and pro-Republican newspapers, where he was labeled "contemptible," "a dangerous demagogue," "eager to use fraud," "shameless," "hypocritical and dangerous," "hollow and untrustworthy," a "self-seeking autocrat," a man with "no respect for the truth."

Beginning in September, Roosevelt campaigned all across the country. He traveled more than ten thousand miles in four weeks and made one or more long speeches a day. On October 7 he set out again, and was in Milwaukee on the fourteenth. At about 8 o'clock at night, he was on his way to a program at a local auditorium. He smiled, waved his hat, and bowed to the people who had gathered on the sidewalk to see him. Some people tried to get close, presumably to shake his hand. One of them had a gun. He was just seven feet away when he shot Roosevelt.

The would-be assassin was John Schrank of New York, a stocky, well-dressed, thirty-six-year-old native of Germany. He and his family had settled in the United States when he was nine.

Schrank had been stalking Roosevelt, from Charleston to Chicago to Milwaukee. At first all he said was, "Any man looking for a third term ought to be shot." Later he said, "I had a dream in which former president McKinley appeared to me. I was told by McKinley in this dream that it was not Czolgosz who murdered him, but Roosevelt." He also said of Roosevelt, "I looked at his plan to start a third party as a danger to his country."

"Everything seemed to happen at once," Roosevelt's secretary, Albert Martin, later said. "There was a flash, the sound of a shot, and I was on the ground with the man. I threw one arm about his neck, and held him fast. . . . I picked the man up and held him where Colonel Roosevelt could see him. 'The poor creature,' said the Colonel."

Schrank was hurried into a police wagon. Hundreds of people followed it, shouting "Kill the brute!" "Get a rope!" "Lynch him!"

Schrank was declared insane and committed to a mental institution, where he lived until his death in 1943.

Roosevelt had been shot in the chest. Luckily, the bullet first hit his steel eyeglass case and the folded fifty-page copy of his speech. The case and papers deflected the bullet slightly, and it missed his lungs and heart. TR said he had not been hurt, and he was continuing on his way when someone noticed a bullet hole in his coat. He opened his coat and discovered that his shirt was covered with blood.

Roosevelt insisted on giving his speech anyway, and spoke for fifty minutes. Henry Cochems introduced him. "The Colonel comes to you in the spirit of a good soldier," he said, "with a bullet in his breast—where, we don't know."

"Friends," Roosevelt said, and asked his audience to be quiet during his talk. "I do not know whether you fully understand that I have just been shot, but it takes more than that to kill a Bull Moose. . . . The bullet is in me now, so that I cannot make a very long speech. But I will try my best."

"It was probably the most dramatic speech, certainly the most dramatic opening, ever made by a great public leader in America," according to Captain Charles Merriam, who was there.

"First of all," Roosevelt said, "I want to say this about myself.

I have altogether too many important things to think of to pay any heed or feel any concern over my own death. . . . I am telling you the literal truth when I say that my concern is for many other things. It is not the least for my own life."

At one point during his talk he opened his jacket, unbuttoned his vest, and showed the audience his bloodied shirt.

His voice was strong when he started his speech, but the emphatic gestures he often made were limited. Then he became unsteady and spoke more softly. A doctor went to him and insisted he stop, but Roosevelt refused. When he was finally done, he was rushed to the hospital. Six surgeons were there, ready for him. The bullet had settled in a rib and didn't need to be removed.

TR gave only two more speeches before the election. While he recovered, to not take advantage of his misfortune, both Taft and Wilson suspended their campaigns.

On the night before the election, several reporters gathered in Oyster Bay to interview Roosevelt. "Going to vote the Democratic ticket on election day, Colonel?" a new reporter asked.

Roosevelt enjoyed a good joke, but he didn't find this one to be funny. His expression turned serious.

The reporter repeated the question.

"I have not come here to answer any idiotic questions," Roosevelt replied.

"What did I do to offend him? What did I do to offend him?" the reporter asked again and again.

The reporter's wife was waiting outside. He had hoped to introduce her to the ex-president, but that never happened.

On November 5 Roosevelt received about 27.5 percent of the votes, and Taft about 23 percent. Wilson, with just under 42 percent, was elected president. Roosevelt had clearly lost the election, but since he and Wilson had many of the same progressive proposals for the country, it was a victory of sorts for TR's ideas.

Roosevelt with his grandson, Kermit Roosevelt, Jr., 1916.

12. Rio Teodoro

During the 1912 election, ugly stories were told about TR. "Roosevelt lies and curses in a most disgusting way," George A. Newett wrote in an October 1912 editorial published in a Michigan newspaper. "He gets drunk, too." To protect his name, Roosevelt sued Newett.

Reporters ran after TR as he hurried to his train at New York City's Grand Central Station to travel to Marquette, Michigan, where the trial was being held. They asked him to comment on the case. "I haven't a thing on earth to say," he answered, "not a single solitary thing."

Just four minutes later they followed a special messenger who delivered a box marked "Medicated Milk" to the train. Perhaps the milk was for Roosevelt. Perhaps the added medication was liquor. The reporters were "pushed back," according to a front-page story in the *New York Times*, "and so the question was unsettled when the train pulled out of the station."

Cabinet officers, his personal doctors, and newspaper reporters all testified in support of the former president. Even Roosevelt testified.

"Isn't it true," Callan O'Loughlin, a reporter for the *Chicago Tribune*, was asked, "that the plaintiff does use intoxicating liquor and occasionally to excess?"

"No reputable Washington correspondent ever for one moment believed such a report, or even talked about it," O'Loughlin answered, "because it was silly."

"He never took a drink with me," Truman Newberry, the ex-secretary of the Navy, testified, "and I'm sure he never did with anyone else."

Roosevelt's old friend Jacob Riis was asked if he had ever heard him curse.

"I have heard him use the expression 'Godfrey,'" Riis answered.

Roosevelt told the court, "No man who knew me ever asked me to take whiskey, because they knew that under no circumstances did I take it. . . . I don't smoke and I don't drink beer, because I dislike smoking and dislike the taste of beer. . . . Mint juleps I very rarely drink. At the White House we had a mint bed, and on the average I may have drunk half a dozen mint juleps a year. . . . During the last fourteen years I do not believe I have drunk whiskey straight or with water more than half a dozen times."

When Roosevelt's lawyers were done prosecuting their case, according to Lawrence Abbott, TR's friend and editor at *The Outlook* magazine, "the defendant actually threw up his hands." Newett was unable to produce a single witness who had heard TR use foul language or seen him drunk. Newett explained that his article was based on common gossip.

"I did not go after the suit for money," Roosevelt told the court. "I made my reputation an issue because I wish once for all during my lifetime thoroughly and comprehensively to deal with these slanders."

Roosevelt won his case, and he was awarded nominal damages— six cents. The estimated cost to defend his honor was forty thousand dollars.

After his victory in court, Roosevelt busied himself speaking at Progressive-Bull Moose Party meetings. One of his favorite subjects was women's suffrage, which he supported. In a speech in 1912 he said, "People say to me, 'Men are different from women.' Yes, but I have never met any differences so great as the differences between some men and other men." And he had great respect for a woman's "traditional" work in the early 1900s. "I have mighty little use for the man who is always declaiming in favor of an eight-hour day for himself," he said, "who does not think anything at all of having a sixteen-hour day for his wife."

TR also indulged his love to hunt. In July 1913 he took his sons Quentin and Archie and their cousin Nicholas Roosevelt on a six-week trip to the U.S. Southwest. From the rim of the Grand Canyon he led them to the Navajo Desert. For long stretches of time the only other living things they saw were lizards and rattlesnakes. At one point during the trip Roosevelt apologized to his sons and their cousin for being too old to keep up with them. Nicholas wrote in his diary that it was TR's weight, not his age, that held him back.

Two months later TR sailed to South America, first to deliver a few speeches and then to hunt and do some scientific exploration for New York's American Museum of Natural History. His son Kermit as well as some botanists and zoologists went with him.

They first visited the settled areas of Brazil, Uruguay, and Argentina. Then they traveled along the Paraguay River to the Amazon River. The areas they explored suffered from torrential rains and extreme heat. The explorers' shoes were quickly torn and rotted. Their skin became covered with bruises, sores, and insect bites. Roosevelt hurt his leg on a rock, and after that he had to be carried.

In the dense jungle Roosevelt and his party encountered poison-ous snakes, man-eating fish, disease-carrying mosquitoes, fire ants, deadly red wasps, and blood-sucking bats. They were often forced to carry their boats and supplies as they encountered rapids and waterfalls. Some of their canoes smashed against the rocks. Two of their native servants drowned.

Then Roosevelt was felled by a fever and couldn't be moved. He told the others to leave him there, but they refused. While everyone waited for him to recover, they went through much of their limited

Theodore Roosevelt pointing to the area of South America he would explore, (1913–1914).

supply of food. If he didn't get better soon, according to his friend William Thayer, "he secretly determined to shoot himself." When he finally felt better, the group moved on. But Roosevelt was so weak he just lay on the bottom of the boat, with a piece of canvas over his head to shade him from the sun. "Too weak from sickness," Thayer wrote, "even to splash water on his face, for he was almost fainting from the muggy heat and the tropical sunshine."

On May 19, 1914, Roosevelt returned to New York.

"There was something lacking in the power of his voice," according to a report in the *New York Times*. "He said he had lost thirty-five pounds. . . . For the first time in his life, it was said, Colonel Roosevelt carried a cane."

Thayer later wrote, "The Brazilian Wilderness stole away ten years of his life," and wondered if his friend regretted the trip. But, he added, "he was a man who wasted no time over regrets. . . . Days were as water that has flowed under the mill."

On the trip they discovered and mapped the Rio da Dúvida, or River of Doubt. In Brazil, to honor TR, they renamed it Rio Roosevelt, but commonly call it Rio Teodoro.

His party brought back more than two thousand specimens of birds, about five hundred mammals, and some reptiles and fish. Many of them were previously unknown to the scientists at the American Museum of Natural History. Among the most interesting of the specimens was the hoatzin, also known as the stinkbird and the canje pheasant, an odd bird with a long neck, a small head, and lizard-like claws on its wings.

Just about everything Theodore Roosevelt did stirred controversy. Some people questioned his findings, but many scientists respected his work. Alaskan and Canadian Arctic explorer Vilhjamur Stefansson spoke of his "competence" and "notable achievements." He described Roosevelt as "the most explorer-minded man I have known." Frank Chapman, the American Museum of Natural History's curator of birds, said, "The Colonel knows more about birds than I do."

"If Mr. Roosevelt's physical troubles prove, as we all wish they may, to be not serious or lasting, he will soon enter the field of politics," the editors of the *New York Times* wrote the day after his return. "One thing we may be sure of, that he will add to the interest of a situation at present a little dull."

He did get back to politics.

He was asked to be the Progressive Party's candidate for governor of New York, but he refused. Nonetheless he worked hard for the party.

In June he campaigned for his friend Gifford Pinchot, the Progressive Party candidate for the Senate from Pennsylvania. Pinchot finished second in a three-man race. TR campaigned for many other Progressive Party candidates. Most of them lost.

"I don't think they can much longer be kept as a party," TR told his daughter Ethel.

In July TR accused New York Republican boss William Barnes of "Republican crookedness" and "corrupt and machine ruled government."

Barnes was furious and sued Roosevelt for libel.

Almost one hundred witnesses testified, including Assistant Secretary of the Navy Franklin Delano Roosevelt, TR's fifth cousin and husband of his niece Eleanor. Theodore Roosevelt also testified. He was questioned over a period of five days. He was not an easy witness. Words seemed to burst from his mouth, and he couldn't keep his hands still.

"Now, if your honor please," Barnes' attorney said at the trial, "I ask that this witness be requested to testify without gesticulation, and in the ordinary and usual way. . . . I do not wish to be eaten up right here and now."

After the more than month-long trial, the jury deliberated for three days. Then finally on Saturday, May 22, they gave their verdict. Theodore Roosevelt was not guilty of libel.

"I will try all my life," Roosevelt told the jurors, "that no one of you will have cause to regret the verdict."

The Roosevelt trial was little more than a natural distraction. There was real trouble abroad and controversy at home. Almost a year earlier, on June 28, 1914, in Bosnia, Austro-Hungarian Archduke Franz Ferdinand had been assassinated. Austrian leaders declared war on Serbia. Germany, Bulgaria, and Turkey—the Central Powers—allied themselves with Austria-Hungary. England, France, and Russia—the Allied Powers—joined with Serbia. This was the "Great War," later called World War I. By its end there would be more than twenty Allied nations fighting the Central Powers. More than nine million solders would be killed in battle. About as many civilians would die of war-caused food shortages and bombings. Soon after the fighting began, President Wilson declared that the United States was "neutral in fact . . . impartial in thought as well as in deed."

In the midst of the Roosevelt-Barnes libel trial, on Friday, May 7, 1915, a huge British ocean liner, the *Lusitania*, was completing its crossing from New York to England when it was attacked and sunk by a German U-boat.

George Kessler of New York was on the ship. "It was a very delightful voyage," he said. "Few people were seasick, and the vessel never pitched or rolled." On a Friday afternoon, "having nothing to do, I leaned over the side of the ship, and to my astonishment I saw

The Lusitania *being hit by torpedoes from a painting.*

a torpedo cleaving the water. . . . Ten seconds later there was a thud at the side of the vessel. She had been hit about midships."

Eleven hundred and ninety-eight passengers and crew members were killed. One hundred and twenty-eight were Americans.

Among the victims was a friend of Roosevelt's, Alfred Vanderbilt, who helped others climb into lifeboats. He could not swim. Nonetheless he gave his life vest to save a young mother.

Roosevelt called the sinking "piracy accompanied by murder on a vaster scale than any old-time pirate had ever practiced before being hung for his misdeeds." He said, "It seems inconceivable that we can refrain from taking action. We owe it not only to humanity but to our own national self-respect."

Roosevelt demanded that the United States enter the war.

President Wilson refused to send American troops into battle.

A few days later Wilson spoke in Philadelphia, his first public speech after the tragedy. "There is such a thing as a man being too proud to fight," he said. "There is such a thing as a nation being so right that it does not need to convince others by force that it is right." He did not even mention the *Lusitania*.

Roosevelt was enraged. He wrote to his son Archie that Wilson was supported by "the solid flubdub and pacifist vote. Every soft creature, every coward and weakling ... the murder of the thousand men, women and children in the *Lusitania* is due solely to Wilson's cowardice and weakness."

On May 13, six days after the sinking of the *Lusitania*, President Wilson insisted the German government apologize, promise to stop attacking non-military vessels, and pay the families of the American victims. Nine months later the Germans finally apologized. They agreed to pay reparations to the victims' families.

"War has been creeping nearer and nearer," Roosevelt said, "and we face it without policy, plan, purpose, or preparation." In July 1915 he said, "Men who are not ready to fight ... are not fit to live in a free democracy." He called Wilson a "lily-livered skunk."

Many in the Republican Party hoped Roosevelt would be a candidate for president in the coming election, but TR refused to run. The Republican candidate was New York Governor Charles Evans Hughes. Wilson ran for reelection as the peace candidate and won.

On February 1, 1917, the German government announced that any ships, peaceful or not, in what it considered the war zone would be attacked. Wilson broke off diplomatic relations with Germany, but despite the urging of members of his Cabinet to take more drastic action, he did not declare war.

Three weeks later the British revealed an intercepted telegram from Arthur Zimmermann, Germany's state secretary for foreign affairs, urging Mexico to go to war with the United States. When the war was won, Germany promised to reward Mexico with territory it had lost to the U.S. in the 1840s.

The Zimmermann telegram sparked Wilson's anger. At last, on April 2, 1917, he asked Congress to declare war on Germany.

"Let us," Roosevelt wrote Senator George Chamberlain of Oregon, "put the American flag at the battle-front in this great world war for Democracy and civilization."

He telegraphed the War Department asking for permission to raise two divisions of soldiers to serve on the front lines. He wrote,

"I don't want to be put in the position of saying to my fellow country-men, 'Go to war.' I want to be in the position of saying: 'Come to the war; I am going with you.' "

"The appearance of an ex-President of the United States carrying the Star-Spangled Banner over a body of American soldiers to the battlefront," wrote the editor of the *Louisville Courier-Journal*, "would glorify us as will nothing else. It will electrify the world."

More than three hundred thousand men volunteered to serve with Roosevelt.

His request was debated in Congress. According to his sister Corinne, it was "one of the most acrimonious debates that ever occurred in the Senate."

The Democrats declared Roosevelt to be unfit for service. The Republicans disagreed. "Oh! for more Roosevelts in this nation," declared Republican Senator Hiram Johnson of California. "Oh! for more men who will stand upon the hustings and go about the country preaching the undiluted Americanism that all of us claim to have! Oh! for more Roosevelts and more divisions of men who will follow Roosevelt!"

On April 15 Roosevelt had his answer. Secretary of War Newton Baker denied his request to lead a volunteer army. Roosevelt was frustrated and bitter. In 1917 and 1918 some ten million American men went to war to fight for the honor of their country, including all four of Roosevelt's sons: Theodore Jr., Kermit, Archie, and Quentin. Alice and Ethel also helped the war effort. But Theodore Roosevelt stayed home.

Newton D. Baker (1871–1937).

I WANT YOU
FOR U.S. ARMY
NEAREST RECRUITING STATION

World War I Army recruiting poster, 1917.

13. "The Lion Is Dead"

In February 1918 Roosevelt collapsed at the Hotel Langdon in New York City. He was drenched in blood. He had an abscess in his thigh and abscesses in his ears, the result of infections contracted during his 1914 exploration in the Brazilian jungle. He was taken to a nearby hospital. By the next morning he was conscious, but he was sure his life was over.

"I don't mind having to die," he told a friend. "I've had my good time. I've had my full life."

He needed an operation on his ears. The surgeon had a dismal record. He told TR that this would be the fifth time he would do the procedure. All the previous four patients had died.

Roosevelt told the doctor, "I should like to see my sons come back from France. But if it can't be, all right, doctor. I don't give a hang!"

"Theodore Roosevelt, listen!" an editorial in one of the New York City newspapers declared. "You must be up and well again. . . . We could not run this world without you."

Remarkably, TR recovered. One week later he was back at work, dictating from his bed a speech he planned to make. But it seemed this was a turning point, a passing of the family torch to the next generation. While TR was bedridden, his children were actively involved in the war.

TR's daughter Alice made cloth bandages for injured soldiers and sold bonds in support of the war effort. According to a magazine report of the time, "She made her handsome home near Cincinnati a general headquarters for war work . . . while the lady of the manor is devoting her time to any feature of the work that demands attention."

TR Jr. served as a lieutenant colonel in the First World War. He was shot in the leg and gassed. "While we experienced hard fighting," he said when he returned home, "most of our time was spent in the small villages back of the lines. Here the men slept in the barns on the hay lofts, with the pigs, cows and rabbits. . . . I slept in a room with a kindly-faced old cow. . . When the cow slept, I slept, and when she was wakeful, I was wakeful, too." According to the homeowner, an old Frenchwoman, it was the soldiers who kept the animals up, not the other way around. She complained to Roosevelt that his men made so much noise that the animals could not sleep.

Later, as his father had been, TR Jr. was assistant secretary of the Navy. He also served as governor of Puerto Rico and governor-general of the Philippines. In 1924 he was the Republican nominee for governor of New York. His cousin Eleanor, FDR's wife, campaigned against him. She followed him around in a car with a teapot on its roof, an effort to link him to the Teapot Dome scandal of Republican President Warren G. Harding. TR Jr. never forgave his cousin. In 1932, when FDR was elected president, he was asked how he was related to FDR and he replied, "fifth cousin about to be removed."

Theodore Jr. rejoined the Army in 1941 as a brigadier general. In June 1944, at 56, he was the oldest soldier in the first wave of the D-Day invasion. In July he died suddenly of a heart attack. He was a commander in the May 1918 Battle of Cantigny, France, the Americans' first offensive attack and first victory. At times he was reckless and led his men ahead of the front lines of battle. For his

BE A U.S. MARINE!
307 Evening Star Building, Washington, D. C.

World War I recruiting poster, 1918.

bravery he was awarded the Distinguished Service Cross and the French Légion d'honneur.

Kermit wanted to be a flier, but he had little training and was competing with a huge number of American applicants, so he joined the British forces. They put him in the machine gun corps. He later transferred to the American Expeditionary Force in France. He was awarded the British Military Cross. Again in World War II Kermit joined the British Army.

He was discharged in May 1941 because of poor health. His poor health was due, in part, to alcohol. Like his uncle Elliot, he suffered from depression. In June 1943 Kermit intentionally shot and killed himself, though at the time it was said he died of a sudden heart attack.

Ethel worked as a nurse near the battlefields in France. According to a magazine report of the time, she "went along to France with her husband when he took up his duties with the ambulance service. It was almost a honeymoon trip and a queer one at that. She went along gladly, dodging submarine peril, and then taking post at her husband's side and giving all possible aid to the young doctor."

For the next almost sixty years she worked as a volunteer nurse for the Red Cross.

Theodore Roosevelt with his daughter Ethel Roosevelt Derby and his grandson Richard, 1915.

Archie was a U.S. infantry officer. At twenty-three, he was the youngest U.S. Army commander in the war. He was shot while leading an attack, and was left injured for fourteen hours on the ground between the Allies' and the enemy's front lines, an area called no-man's-land. For his bravery he was awarded the French War Cross and sent home to recover. He served in the Second World War and at forty-seven he was the oldest U.S. Army battle commander.

Quentin, Roosevelt's youngest son, was an American airman. Just after Theodore Jr. and Archie went off to France, there was a large rally for the troops at Roosevelt's Long Island house. An Army airplane flew over Oyster Bay doing daring dips and turns. The crowd was thrilled. Several days later TR found out that Quentin had been flying the airplane.

Lieutenant Quentin Roosevelt (1897–1918).

Soon after that, Quentin shipped overseas.

He was in France in 1918 when someone complimented the Roosevelt sons for their patriotism. All four of them were in the war. "Well," Quentin said, "we boys thought that it was up to us to practice what father preached."

On July 5, 1918, he had his first air encounter with the enemy, who was flying just a little over two hundred yards above Quentin's airplane. "I'm free to confess," he wrote to his fiancée, Flora Payne Whitney, "that I was scared blue." He survived that encounter. On July 10 he shot down an enemy plane. On July 15 he was in the air again. He chased enemy aircraft into a trap of of ground fire. "Bullets were flying everywhere," according to a pilot who survived the attack. There "was a continuous tat, tat, tat of the machine guns."

Quentin Roosevelt did not survive the battle.

According to Quentin's commander, Captain Eddie Rickenbacker, "As President Roosevelt's son he had rather a difficult task to fit himself in. . . . Everyone who met him for the first time expected him to have the airs and superciliousness of a spoiled boy. This notion was quickly lost after the first glimpse one had of Quentin. Gay, hearty and absolutely square in everything he said or did, Quentin Roosevelt was one of the most popular fellows in the group. We loved him purely for his own natural self."

On July 17, 1918, Roosevelt was notified that his son had been killed.

TR walked back and forth on the front porch of his Oyster Bay home. "Mrs. Roosevelt," he said in anguish. "How am I going to break it to her?"

General Pershing cabled the Roosevelts that if they wanted, Quentin's body would be sent home for burial.

"So far as our son Quentin is concerned," Roosevelt wrote back, "we have always believed that 'Where the tree falls, there let it lie.' . . . After the war is over Mrs. Roosevelt and I intend to visit the grave and then to have a small stone put up."

In August a neighbor wrote to Roosevelt suggesting that a monument be erected in Oyster Bay for Quentin. "That is a very nice letter of yours," Roosevelt wrote back, "but I do not think it would be advisable. . . . Of course, individually, our loss is irreparable but to the country he is simply one among many gallant boys who gave their lives for the great Cause."

Roosevelt was a changed man after the death of Quentin. According to his friend Hermann Hagedorn, "The boy in him had died."

The fortunes of war shifted. The Allies seemed to be on the road to victory, and talk turned to politics. Leaders of the New York Republican Party wanted Roosevelt to run for governor. He wasn't interested. He was focused on national politics.

In July and August 1918, huge numbers of American troops arrived on the battlefields of Europe. By the end of September, American General John J. Pershing had more than one million American soldiers under his command. The surge of American troops made the difference in the war. The fighting stopped on the eleventh hour of the eleventh day of the eleventh month— November 11, 1918. On that day the enemies in the Great War agreed to negotiate the terms of a peace agreement.

Throughout the United States and Western Europe, people crowded the streets to celebrate.

There was peace in Europe, but not at home. There was renewed tension between business and organized labor. There was also racial tension. Three hundred sixty-seven thousand African Americans had been drafted to serve in the American armed forces. Now they were returning home, educated and trained in the use of firearms. Many whites became militant—murderously so—out of a supposed fear that African Americans would rebel against their second-class status in the U.S. In 1918 more than fifty blacks were lynched. There were race riots in Pennsylvania. The next year there were more lynchings and race riots.

The nation needed a strong and compassionate leader.

Roosevelt was still a relatively young man, just sixty. He was asked if he planned to run for the Republican nomination for president in the coming 1920 election.

"Yes," Roosevelt answered, "I will run if the people want me, but only if they want me." He added that he would not actively campaign for the nomination. He would take it if the party came to him. He said, "It would be worthless on any other basis."

TR was relatively young, but he wasn't in good health.

On November 11, the very day the war ended, Roosevelt was again taken to the hospital, this time with inflammatory rheumatism, apparently also caused by an infection he contracted during his South American safari. His arm was terribly swollen. He stayed in the hospital for six weeks.

"There was no serious apprehension about his health," his sister Corinne later wrote, "except for a brief thirty-six hours when he was threatened with pneumonia."

When Corinne visited him, he told her, "Well, anyway, no matter what comes, I have kept the promise that I made to myself when I was twenty-one . . . that I would work *up to the hilt* until I was sixty, and I have done it."

On Christmas morning Roosevelt left the hospital and returned to his home, Sagamore Hill in Oyster Bay. He was pale and weak. His children and grandchildren joined him and Edith for Christmas dinner.

He was soon at work again. He dictated articles and responses to the many letters sent to him. He made plans for a trip in March to the Gulf of Mexico to hunt devilfish.

On Saturday, January 4, Edith called James Amos, the African-American aide who had been with him since his White House days. She asked him to come to Sagamore Hill to help. "His face bore a tired expression," Amos said later. "There was a look of weariness in his eyes."

On Sunday Ethel wrote to Kermit that their father was having a "horrid, painful time." Nonetheless he worked in bed on some magazine articles. He kept busy until eleven o'clock that night.

"Put out the light," he told Amos.

Those were his last words.

In the morning, at two o'clock, Mrs. Roosevelt looked in on him. He was sleeping. At four o'clock Amos, who was sleeping in the next room, thought Roosevelt's breathing had what he described as a "hollow sound." He called the nurse who was in the house.

Edith heard the commotion and rushed to her husband's side. "Theodore, darling!" she said. But he didn't reply.

She called the doctor, who pronounced him dead. Roosevelt died of a pulmonary embolism, a blood clot that traveled through his arteries to his lungs, where it stopped his blood from circulating.

The family members living nearby were called. Archie cabled those living far away, "The Lion is dead."

14. Remembering Roosevelt

On Monday morning, January 6, relatives and friends of Theodore and Edith Roosevelt gathered at the house in Oyster Bay. They consoled Edith and helped plan the funeral. Thousands of telegrams, cables, and letters of sympathy arrived. Late that afternoon three airplanes flew overhead. In memory of the fallen president, the airmen aboard dropped laurel wreaths into the trees that surrounded the house.

An airman dropping a wreath on the Roosevelt home, January 6, 1919.

"Boy! There's nothing like him in history." Art and caption from the St. Paul "Pioneer Press," c. 1909.

"Please accept my heartfelt sympathy in the death of your distinguished husband," President Wilson wrote to Mrs. Roosevelt, "the news of which has shocked me very much."

"I am shocked to hear the sad news," former president Taft wrote. "We have lost a great patriotic American, a great world figure, the most commanding personality in our public life since Lincoln. I mourn his going as a personal loss."

The Czechoslovak National Council mourned "the loss of so ardent a supporter of oppressed peoples."

"With the death of ex-President Roosevelt," the *New York Times* reported the next day, the Republican Party had lost its greatest spokesperson. "Among party leaders today it was conceded that if Colonel Roosevelt had lived, he undoubtedly would have had the nomination for the Presidency."

Theodore Roosevelt's funeral was Wednesday afternoon, January 8, at Christ Episcopal Church in Oyster Bay.

It was a dark, overcast day. Snow fell through the morning.

Just before one o'clock, Father G. E. Talmage, the Roosevelts' minister, entered the church. He was followed by six pallbearers carrying the coffin, which was draped in an American flag. There was a wreath on top of the flag, along with two Rough Riders banners.

When the short service ended, the church bell rang once. Then Roosevelt's remains were taken to the nearby Young's Memorial Cemetery for burial.

Former and future presidents Taft and Harding were at the service, along with Vice President Marshall, Governor Al Smith of New York, and U.S. and foreign dignitaries. Father J. J. Curran of Wilkes-Barre, Pennsylvania, who had helped Roosevelt settle the 1902 coal strike, was there, too.

"I came," Curran said, "to pay my tribute to the best man that ever lived."

"His country was the ruling, mastering passion of his life from the beginning even unto the end," Senator Henry Cabot Lodge said of his close friend. He spoke of Roosevelt's "intense energy . . . powerful, well-trained, ever-active mind," great storehouse of information, and abilities as a leader and writer. As a public speaker, he said, TR was "one of the most effective in all our history."

"He was one of the world's great figures, conspicuous, dominating, always intensely interesting," declared a *New York Times* editorial. "He put the stamp of his genius upon the history of his country."

"Yesterday, he seemed one who embodied Life to the utmost," William Roscoe Thayer, his friend of forty years, remembered. "With the assured step of one whom nothing can frighten or surprise, he walked our earth. . . . Happy we who had such a friend! Happy the American Republic which bore such a son!"

He was a supremely talented man. He was a great president who ably led the nation through turbulent times. He was a great American.

A memorial drawing published in the Harrisburg Telegraph.

IMPORTANT DATES

1858	Born in New York City, October 27.
1865	Watches Lincoln's funeral procession though New York City.
1878	His father, Theodore Roosevelt Sr., dies, February 9.
1880	Graduates from Harvard College.
	Marries Alice Hathaway Lee in Brookline, Massachusetts, October 27.
1881	Elected New York assemblyman, November 8.
1880–1882	Attends Columbia Law School.
1882	His first book, *The Naval War of 1812*, is published.
1884	His daughter Alice Lee is born, February 12.
	Both his mother and wife die, February 14.
1886	Loses election for mayor of New York City, November 2.
	Marries Edith Kermit Carow, December 2.
	They will have five children.
1889	Appointed to the U.S. Civil Service Commission.
1895	Appointed New York police commissioner.
1897	Appointed assistant secretary of the Navy.
1898	With Dr. Leonard Wood, forms the First Volunteer Cavalry, the Rough Riders.
	Leads the charge in the Battle of San Juan Hill, July 1.
	Elected governor of New York, November 8.
1900	Elected vice president, November 6.
1901	President McKinley dies. Roosevelt succeeds him as president, September 14.
1902	Panama Canal Act passes, June.
	Arbitrates settlement in coal strike, October.
	Venezuela debt crises settled, December.
1903	Settles Alaska boundary dispute with Canada.
	Panama breaks away from Colombia and is recognized by U.S.

1904	Elected president, November 8.
1905	Negotiates Japanese–Russian peace treaty.
	Gives his niece Eleanor in marriage to future president Franklin Delano Roosevelt, a distant cousin, March 17.
1906	At the White House, gives his daughter Alice in marriage to Congressman Nicholas Longworth of Ohio, February 17.
	Awarded Nobel Peace Prize; he accepts the award in 1910 while in Europe.
1909	Leaves for African safari, March 23.
1910	Safari ends in Khartoum, March 14. Returns to New York, June 18.
1912	Announces his intention to be a candidate for president, February 24.
	Nominated as a candidate for president by newly formed Progressive Party, August 7.
	Defeated by Woodrow Wilson, November 5.
1913	Leaves for South America, October 4.
1914	Returns to New York, May 19.
1918	Youngest son, Quentin, killed in France, July 14.
1919	Dies in New York, January 6.

1904 cartoon from New York World.

SOURCE NOTES

Preface: Colonel Theodore Roosevelt

p. v   "Father always wanted . . . at every funeral." Cook, p. 167.

p. v   "If I were asked . . . That's good enough." Pringle, p. 589.

1. The Cowboy President

p. 2   "Expositions are time-keepers . . . not those of war." Lossing, volume VI, pp. 33–36.

p. 4   "So rapidly . . . without moving a muscle." *New York Times*, September 8, 1901, p. 2. The witness was Charles J. P. Lucas of Cambridge, Massachusetts. When the shots were fired he was in line to meet McKinley, just four people behind Czolgosz.

p. 4   "Be careful how you tell her. . . . Don't let them hurt him." H. Wayne Morgan, p. 521.

p. 4   "I am not badly hurt, I assure you." *New York Times*, September 7, 1901, p. 1.

p. 4   "I done my duty." http://en.wikipedia.org/wiki/Assassination_of_William_McKinley.

p. 4   "The President passed . . . symptoms have developed." H. Wayne Morgan, p. 523.

p. 4   "The President is sinking." Ibid. p. 524.

p. 5   "William, William, don't you know me?" Ibid., p. 402.

p. 5   "Good-bye . . . not ours." *New York Times*, September 14, 1901, p. 1.

p. 5   "I told . . . of the United States!" Morris, *Theodore Rex*, p. 30.

p. 5   "short, nearsighted . . . high pitched voice." Martin, p. 690.

p. 5   "human steam engine." Donald, p. 40.

2. Teedie

p. 7   The family first dropped the "Van" in their name and became Rosenvelt, then Rosavelt, and in 1750, Roosevelt. The early Roosevelts worked in real estate, trade, and banking. Among the family's first real-estate dealings was Klaes Van Rosenvelt's purchase in 1652 of a forty-eight-acre farm covering much of present-day midtown Manhattan including the site of the Empire State Building.

p. 7   By the time Roosevelt was president, his birthplace no longer belonged to his family. In 1903 it was raided by New York City detectives. It was a suspected gamblers den. The men in the house were playing checkers. The police found a suspicious pile of ashes in the fireplace and above it, on a handwritten card, "President Roosevelt Was Born in This House." Drinker and Mowbray, p. 452.

p. 7   "City of Immigrants." Burrows and Wallace, p. 736.

p. 8   Atlanta wasn't established until 1847, at the intersection of two railroad lines.

p. 8   According to Cook, p. 28, in a temper fit, Mittie's half brother Daniel Stewart Elliot killed his shadow slave.

p. 8   "black, fine hair . . . a rose, tint." Robinson, p. 19.

p. 9   "The finest man . . . and the happiest." James Morgan, pp. 10–11.

p. 10   "sweet and pretty . . . ever seen." Miller, p. 29.

p. 10   Noisy and fussy. Pringle, p. 3.

pp. 10–11   "his advice . . . especially becoming." Robinson, p. 26.

p. 12   "No discrimination . . . the funeral procession." Davis, p. 13.

p. 13   "most thoroughly understand and appreciate Lincoln." Miller, p. 19.

p. 13   "I was a . . . I could breathe." Roosevelt, p. 14.

p. 13   "a kind of . . . *make my body*." Robinson, p. 50.

p. 13   "For many years . . . the strenuous life." Ibid.

pp. 13–14   "One may well . . . ever performed again." Ibid., p. 51.

p. 14   "We used to sit . . . to be continued." Ibid., p. 2.

p. 14   "I remember distinctly . . . on a slab of wood." Roosevelt, p. 14.

p. 14   "the loss to science." Pringle, p. 17.

p. 15   "We were given . . . on horseback." Lewis, p. 38.

p. 15   "He was always . . . in later life." Lewis, p. 36.

p. 15   "Other boys asked . . . the *nature* of the force." Riis, p. 407.

p. 15   "It puzzled me . . . entirely new world," Roosevelt, p. 19.

pp. 15–17   "I was sick . . . same thing as yesterday." Hagedorn, pp. 31–35.

p. 17   "We want to . . . Ever yours, T. Roosevelt." Ibid., p. 35.

p. 17   "God's country." Ibid., p. 36.

p. 17   "This trip formed . . . of my education." Roosevelt, p. 20.

p. 17   "well-meaning maid . . . my wash kit." Ibid., p. 21.

p. 17   "Teedie and Father . . . fun for him." Robinson, p. 56.

KAISERIN AUGUSTE VICTORIA

p. 17	"I think I have enjoyed . . . several hundred birds with it." Ibid., p. 67.
p. 18	"We went into . . . exploring mummy pits." Ibid., p. 57.
p. 18	"Health; good . . . a dead bat." Ibid., p. 84.
p. 19	"The young man . . . on Natural History." Morris, *The Rise of Theodore Roosevelt*, p. 75.

3. As Plain as a Spruce Board

p. 20	"We hitched up . . . expressing his opinion." Hagedorn, p. 61.
p. 20	"as plain as . . . square as a brick." Russell, pp. 95–96.
p. 20	"he was almost . . . destined for greatness." Ibid., p. 95.
p. 21	"Foul! . . . He didn't hear!" James Morgan, p. 24.
p. 21	"he was no grind . . . but intense way." Thayer, pp. 16–17.
p. 22	"showed unusual energy . . . and tenacity." Drinker and Mowbray, pp. 24–25.
p. 22	"I think there . . . *the man's name*." Miller, p. 100.
p. 22	"I left college . . . to which I belonged." Roosevelt, p. 28.
p. 23	"mad with pain." Morris, *The Rise of Theodore Roosevelt*, p. 94.
p. 23	"I kissed the . . . his loving smile." Ibid., p. 95.
p. 23	"What living and loving . . . very bitter moments." Robinson, p. 106.
p. 23	"I saw her sweet, fair young face." Pringle, p. 40.
p. 23	"See that girl? . . . to marry her." Pringle, p. 42; Grondahl, p. 57.
p. 23	In Grondahl, the friend is identified as Martha Cowdin.
p. 24	"danced the soles off her shoes." Miller, p. 104; Morris, *The Rise of Theodore Roosevelt*, p. 135.
p. 24	"I fed her . . . world again." Miller, p. 113.
p. 25	"seemed to grasp everything instantly." Pringle, p. 55.
p. 25	"Some of the teaching . . . is apt to feel." Roosevelt, p. 55.
p. 25	"a man's first . . . object of my career." Roosevelt, pp. 55–56.
pp. 25–26	"politics were 'low' . . . rough and tumble." Roosevelt, p. 57.

4. "My Heart's Dearest"

p. 27	"I joined . . . a good time." Riis, p. 49.
p. 27	"the most indiscreet guy I ever met." Chessman, p. 31.
p. 28	"swindler" and "beyond reproach." Miller, p. 133.
p. 28	"unwise." Ibid., p. 136.
p. 28	"an excellent one . . . of telling events." *New York Times*, June 5, 1882, p. 2.
p. 28	"absolutely deserted." James Morgan, p. 44.
p. 28	"That was my first real . . . men as they are." Ibid., p. 45.
p. 29	"I am so delighted." Miller, p. 149.
p. 29	"We shot him and took his rattles," Ibid., p. 151.
p. 31	"By Godfrey, but this is fun." Morris, *The Rise of Theodore Roosevelt*, p. 220; Miller, p. 151.
p. 31	"I dismounted . . . your loving, Thee." Miller, p. 152.
p. 32	"Mother is dying . . . curse on this house." Miller, p. 155; Marschall, p. 49.
p. 32	"There is a curse on this house." Pringle, p. 51.
p. 33	"dazed . . . what he does or says." Morris, *The Rise of Theodore Roosevelt*, p. 243.
p. 33	"She was beautiful . . . from my life for ever." Pringle, p. 51.

5. Assemblyman, Rancher, Police Commissioner, Navy Man

p. 35	"It was a grim . . . cease from working." Hagedorn, p. 96. Roosevelt wrote this in a letter to his friend the Maine guide Bill Sewall.
p. 35	"that dentificial young man with more teeth than brains." Ibid.
p. 36	He insisted on being called "Mr. Roosevelt." Miller, p. 164.
p. 36	"I do not believe . . . of instant decision." Roosevelt, p. 96.
p. 36	"We led a free . . . joy of living." Miller, p. 164.

p. 36   "The only time . . . He was senseless."
Roosevelt, pp. 124–125.

p. 37   "There were all . . . ceased to be afraid."
Wagenknecht, p. 23.

p. 37   "We would follow . . . he turned to us."
Lewis, p. 80.

p. 38   "a gouty old man . . . cultured but scholarly."
Wagenknecht, p. 167.

p. 38   "love of his life." Ibid., p. 166.

p. 38   "They were very cruel about it and I was
terrible sensitive." Miller, p. 192.

p. 38   "We might have to ask her for money." Ibid.,
p. 194.

p. 39   "I shall probably never be in politics again."
Ibid., p. 197.

p. 39   "take the boys in out of the cold to warm
their toes." Lewis, p. 85.

p. 40   "I saw a steady . . . in New York
to-day." James Morgan, pp. 89–90.

p. 40   "Go back to your beat, now." Ibid.,
p. 93.

p. 41   "very pretty." Pringle, p. 138.

p. 41   "Did the police . . . they loved him." Riis,
p. 145.

p. 41   "These midnight rambles . . . swarming
millions." Hagedorn, p. 173.

p. 41   "Of course I told them . . . must be
maintained." Marschall, p. 87.

p. 41   "Select thirty good . . . report to me." James
Morgan, p. 101.

p. 42   "mute and stiff as statues." Ibid.,
p. 102.

p. 42   "I would rather . . . by violating them." Ibid.,
pp.112–113.

p. 42   "No nation can . . . an armed hand." Miller,
p. 255.

p. 42   That the navy had just ninety ships and
that more than half of them were either not
water-ready or out of commission is from
Lewis, p. 122.

p. 42   "Gentlemen . . . about building the ark."
James Morgan, p. 109.

p. 43   "FOUL PLAY!" . . . "AN ENEMY'S INFERNAL
MACHINE." Miller, p. 266.

p. 43   "Everybody in Washington . . . the front
tomorrow." Lewis, p. 134.

6. Rough Rider, Governor, Vice President

p. 45   "Every man who . . . the pain, and
the danger." Wagenknecht, p. 249.

p. 45   "We drew recruits . . . one in ten."
Roosevelt's *The Rough Riders,*
pp. 9–10.

p. 46   "Happy Jack . . . bronco buster." Lewis,
p. 137.

p. 46   "Tough Ike . . . Pork Chop." Miller, p. 277.

p. 46   "Teddy's Terrors." Thayer, p. 125.

p. 46   The origin of the term "Rough Riders" is
from Lewis, p. 136.

p. 46   "The men held . . . bulldog courage." Miller,
p. 303.

p. 47   "We had a bully . . . to wounded here."
Wagenknecht, p. 22.

p. 48   "Outside of my . . . else on earth." James
Morgan, p. 149.

p. 48   "Who is in there? . . . merely a senator?"
Henderson, p. 130.

p. 48   "He was the . . . in America." Thayer, p. 129.

p. 48   Of the total 1,350,000 votes cast in New
York's 1898 election for governor, Roosevelt
won by just 17,000 votes. Lewis, p. 152.

p. 49   "I am proud . . . cannot threaten me."
Hagedorn, p. 222.

p. 49   "did just what he pleased." Miller, p. 323.

p. 49   "I don't want . . . to bury him." Ibid.,
p. 335.

p. 49   "Under no circumstances . . . nomination for
the Vice-Presidency." James Morgan, p. 159.

p. 50   "I had to take it . . . long as I live." Iglehart,
p. 159.

p. 50   "We have the best . . . great as governor."
Drinker and Mowbray, p. 161.

p. 50   The number of miles Roosevelt traveled in
the 1900 campaign, along with the number
of speeches he made and the number of
people he reached, are from Pringle, p. 225;
Stratemeyer, p. 208; and James Morgan, p. 161.

p. 51   "I've read this . . . it is ever new." Russell,
p. 357.

p. 51   "But he was smiling . . . missed it for
anything.' " James Morgan, p. 162; Russell,
p. 178.

p. 51   "a bully time." Russell, p. 178.

p. 51   In 1900 *The Wonderful Wizard of Oz* by
L. Frank Baum was first published, and
according to some scholars the story is an
allegory for the gold and silver debate. In
the book Dorothy wore silver, not ruby,
slippers and walked on the Yellow Brick
Road, the golden road, to the Emerald City,
a veiled reference to greenbacks—paper
money. The wizard who ruled Oz used deceit
and trickery to maintain his power, perhaps
a comment on the methods of the railroad
and oil barons of the era.

p. 51   "We belong to . . . an ever-increasing share."
Miller, p. 345.

7. President

p. 53   "In this hour . . . our beloved country."
Hagedorn, p. 234.

pp. 53–54   "shook and trembled . . . smoke, and smell."
Time-Life, p. 228.

pp. 55–56   "particularly admirable . . . day after day."
New York Times, April 26, 1908, pp. 1–4.

p. 56   "I curled up . . . Theodore was the spinner."
Wagenknecht, p. 6.

p. 56 "Almost always . . . was personally recognized." Robinson, p. 215.

p. 56 "for an egotistical inability . . . open minded of men." Ibid., p. 249.

p. 56 "What have you . . . the work shines." Iglehart, pp. 60–61.

pp. 56–57 "The door of . . . as for the rich." James Morgan, p. 184.

p. 57 "I dined with . . . of his family." David, p. 202.

p. 57 "damnable outrage" and "President Roosevelt . . . worse than a crime." Davis, p. 207.

p. 58 He did not support easier access for blacks to the voting booth. He did not appoint a great number of blacks to federal jobs. Mowry, pp. 165–166.

pp. 58–59 "All children . . . they possibly can." Banks, p. 157.

p. 59 "took delight in . . . walking on stilts." Teichmann, p. 30.

p. 59 "Nothing . . . no place with them." Thayer, p. 259.

p. 60 "I can be president . . . I cannot possibly do both." New York Times Book Review, November 18, 2007, p. 14.

p. 60 "Poor TR Jr. . . . as his father would." Miller, p. 269, n.

p. 60 "In his facial . . . much of his father." Iglehart, p. 259.

p. 60 "looks so much . . . soften my heart." Iglehart, p. 265.

p. 60 "the apple of . . . as a mature woman." Ibid., p. 272.

p. 60 "It was the most . . . romance of the saddle." Washington Post, February 16, 1913, p. ES8.

p. 60 "A bright eye . . . a kindly spirit." Iglehart, pp. 263–264.

p. 61 "possessed evidences of the highest genius." Iglehart, p. 268.

p. 61 "I see him occasionally . . . his family life." Wikipedia, "Quentin Roosevelt."

p. 61 "Well . . . what father preached." Iglehart, p. 269.

p. 61 "to pelt the . . . and nicely thrown." New York Times, January 12, 1904, p. 1.

p. 61 "A pair of red-headed woodpeckers . . . White House grounds." James Morgan, p. 253.

pp. 61–62 "The hearty, wholesome . . . lead the chorus." Ibid., p. 254.

p. 62 "I used to box . . . box any longer." Russell, p. 225.

p. 62 "I give you my word . . . a chance with him." Ibid., p. 226.

p. 62 "There is nothing more to say about the matter." Ibid., p. 227.

p. 63 "I was counted . . . a couple of hours." Iglehart, pp. 247–248.

p. 63 "I have met Mr. Roosevelt . . . and righteous arm." Riis, pp. 320–321.

p. 63 "I eat too much." Wagenknecht, p. 25.

p. 63 "eating like a machine." Ibid., p. 26.

p. 64 "Colonel Roosevelt . . . good-sized revolver." New York Times, October 15, 1912, p. 3.

pp. 64–65 "Of course, I am excited . . . rendered to his country." Robinson, p. 217.

p. 65 "wise custom . . . nomination for another." Thayer, p 308.

p. 66 "How I wished Father could have been here to see it too!" Miller, p. 22.

8. Trustbuster

p. 67 "Give every man . . . harm any one." Drinker and Mowbray, p. 453.

p. 69 "A calamity threatened . . . an enemy's army." Thayer, p. 243.

p. 69 "criminal" and "If it wasn't . . . of that window." Martin, p. 672.

p. 69 "Some men . . . Both are wrong." Riis, p. 380.

p. 70 "I don't think . . . to use it." Miller, p. 423.

p. 71 "The quality of sharing . . . times of sorrow." Robinson, p. 156.

p. 71 Franklin Roosevelt was his wife Eleanor's fifth cousin once removed.

p. 71 "We are greatly rejoiced . . . the true woman." Cook, p. 164.

pp. 71–72 "Your uncle and I . . . arrangements for it." Ibid., p. 165.

p. 72 "Who giveth this . . . I do." Ibid., p. 166.

pp. 72–73 "It was a glorious . . . pearl-gray gloves." New York Times, February 18, 1906, p. 1.

9. The Big Stick

p. 75 "I urged him . . . all the time." Wagenknecht, p. 247.

p. 75 "This country needs a war." Pringle, p. 167.

p. 75 "this chip-on-the-shoulder attitude . . . ruffian and a bully." Pringle, pp. 167–168.

p. 75 "The victories of . . . war are greater." Wagenknecht, p. 248.

p. 76 "This nation most . . . war breaks out." Lossing, volume 7, pp. 485–486.

p. 76 "is very small . . . a thoroughly efficient navy." Arizona Republican, December 3, 1902, p. 8.

p. 78 "The fairness . . . and determine issues." Pringle, p. 292.

p. 79 "Perdicaris alive or Raisuli dead." Miller, p. 439.

p. 79 "be polite and . . . knock their heads together." Wagenknecht, p. 268.

p. 79 "wicked absurdity." Miller, p. 479.

p. 80 "He can lead . . . sees the wrong." Russell, p. 191.

p. 80 "I have had a corking time." Ibid., p. 219.

10. African Safari and Welcome Home

p. 81   "Poor old boy! . . . in tennis costume appear." Pringle, pp. 503–504.

p. 82   Taft was elected with some 1,269,000 more votes than William Jennings Bryan, his Democratic opponent. In 1904 Roosevelt was elected with some 2,543,000 more votes than his opponent, Alton Parker.

p. 82   "I knew there would . . . out of office." Lewis, p. 301.

pp. 82–83   "Kermit and I . . . for both purposes." Lewis, p. 303.

p. 84   "I have taken . . . until he dropped him." "Well, we found . . . to read Balzac." *New York Times*, January 8, 1919, p. 5.

pp. 84–85   "very near squeak . . . extinct in a few years." *New York Times*, January 8, 1919, p. 5.

p. 85   "not just wrong . . . contemptible and wicked." Wagenknecht, p. 18.

p. 85   "Two days ago . . . them being mauled." Ibid., p. 20.

p. 86   "Oh, sweetest of all . . . last twenty-three years." Miller, pp. 499–500.

p. 86   "My friend Roosevelt . . . American citizen." Lewis, p. 313.

p. 87   "Oh, bully . . . in the saddle, too." Drinker and Mowbray, p. 361.

p. 87   "red-blooded, warm-hearted . . . President for life." Ibid., pp. 382–383.

p. 88   In 1919 the ship that brought the Roosevelts home in 1910, the *Kaiserin Auguste Victoria*, would make five trips across the Atlantic to bring American troops home from the war in Europe.

p. 88   "Bully." *Chronicle of America*, p. 567.

p. 88   "He himself was . . . through his native city." *New York Times*, June 19, 1910, p. 1.

p. 88   "The Colonel waved . . . Oh, it's simply great!' " Ibid., p. 2.

p. 88   "I'm so glad . . . meaning of the words." Ibid.

pp. 88–89   "Colonel Roosevelt knew . . . orders from the boss?' " Iglehart, pp. 281–282.

p. 89   *That type* of crowd . . . rotten eggs at me." Robinson, p. 262.

11. Bull Moose

p. 91   "I have thoroughly . . . among people I love." McSpadden, p. 163.

pp. 91–92   "My method . . . not worked smoothly." Graff, p. 352.

p. 92   "neurotics" . . . "men of cold heart and narrow mind" . . . "dull timidity and dull inaction." Martin, p. 697.

p. 92   "The fight is on." Miller, p. 522.

p. 92   "vanity and egotism . . . why not for life." O'Toole, p. 170.

p. 92   "Like a bull moose," *Time*, July 3, 2006, p. 76.

p. 93   "Baltimore unmakes him . . . sure of his defeat." *New York Times*, July 3, 1912, p. 10.

p. 94   "I hope we shall win . . . we battle for the Lord." www.ssa.gov/history/trspeech.html.

p. 95   "It is idle . . . are most proud." *New York Times*, August 10, 1912, p. 2.

p. 95   "I would rather . . . any other presidential candidate." Drinker and Mowbray, p. 411.

p. 95   "contemptible . . . no respect for the truth." Abbott, pp. 280–281.

pp. 95–96   "Any man looking . . . danger to his country." *New York Times*, October 15, 1912, p. 2.

p. 96   "Everything seemed . . . said the Colonel." Ibid.

p. 96   "Kill the brute!" . . . "Lynch him!" Ibid.

p. 96   "The Colonel comes . . . we don't know." Ibid., p. 8.

p. 96   "Friends . . . try my best." Ibid., p. 8.

p. 96   "It was probably . . . leader in America," Russell, p. 246.

pp. 96–97   "First of all . . . my own life." *New York Times*, October 15, 1912, p. 8.

p. 97   "Going to vote . . . to offend him?" *New York Times*, January 12, 1919, p. 69.

12. Rio Teodoro

p. 99   "Roosevelt lies and curses . . . gets drunk, too." O'Toole, p. 239.

p. 99   "I haven't a thing . . . out of the station." *New York Times*, May 25, 1913, p. 1.

pp. 99–100   "Isn't it true . . . with anyone else." *New York Times*, May 29, 1913, p. 1.

p. 100   "I have heard him use the expression 'Godfrey.' " O'Toole, p. 241.

p. 100   "No man who knew me . . . half a dozen times." *New York Times*, May 28, 1913, p. 2.

p. 100   "the defendant actually . . . with these slanders." Abbott, pp. 283–284.

pp. 100–101   "People say to me . . . and other men." Morris, *Colonel Roosevelt*, p. 237.

p. 101   "I have mighty . . . for his wife." Wagenknecht, p. 89

p. 102   "he secretly determined to shoot himself . . . tropical sunshine." Thayer, p. 393.

p. 102   "There was something . . . carried a cane." *New York Times*, May 20, 1914, p. 1.

p. 102   "The Brazilian Wilderness . . . under the mill." Thayer, p. 394.

p. 103   "competence . . . birds than I do." Drinker and Mowbray, 427–428.

p. 103   "If Mr. Roosevelt's . . . at present a little dull." *New York Times*, May 20, 1914, p. 12.

p. 103   "I don't think they can much longer be kept as a party." Miller, p. 542.

p. 103   "Republican crookedness . . . machine ruled government." Pringle, pp. 575–576.

p. 104   "Now, if your honor . . . right here and now." Wagenknecht, p. 9.

p. 104 "I will try . . . regret the verdict." Morris, *Colonel Roosevelt*, p. 424.

p. 104 "neutral in fact . . . as in deed." *Chronicle of America*, p. 584.

pp. 104–105 "It was a very . . . hit about midships." *New York Times*, May 16, 1915, p. 5.

p. 105 "piracy accompanied by . . . for his misdeeds." *New York Times*, May 17, 1915, p. 2.

p. 105 "It seems inconceivable . . . national self-respect." Morris, *Colonel Roosevelt*, p. 419.

p. 105 "There is such . . . that it is right." Lewis, p. 462.

pp. 105–106 "the solid flubdub . . . cowardice and weakness." Morris, *Colonel Roosevelt*, pp. 420–421.

p. 106 "War has been creeping . . . purpose, or preparation." Robinson, p. 309.

p. 106 "Men who are . . . in a free democracy." Drinker and Mowbray, p. 430.

p. 106 "lily-livered skunk." Morris, *Colonel Roosevelt*, p. 480.

p. 106 "Let us . . . Democracy and civilization." Robinson, p. 327.

p. 107 "I don't want . . . going with you.' " Henderson, p. 214.

p. 107 "The appearance of . . . electrify the world." Henderson, p. 217.

p. 107 According to Lewis, p. 467, more than three hundred thousand men volunteered to join Roosevelt.

p. 107 "one of the most acrimonious debates that ever occurred in the Senate." Robinson, p. 328.

p. 107 "Oh! for more Roosevelts . . . who will follow Roosevelt!" Ibid., p. 329.

13. "The Lion Is Dead"

p. 109 "I don't mind . . . don't give a hang!" Hagedorn, p. 379.

p. 109 "Theodore Roosevelt, listen! . . . world without you." Ibid., p. 380.

p. 110 "She made her . . . demands attention." *Indianapolis Star Magazine*, July 15, 1917, p. SM5.

p. 110 "While we experienced . . . I was wakeful, too." Iglehart, pp. 261–262.

p. 110 "fifth cousin about to be removed." http:en. wikipedia.org/wiki/Theodore_Roosevelt_Jr.

p. 112 "went along . . . aid to the young doctor." Ibid.

p. 113 "I'm free to confess . . . scared blue." O'Toole, p. 387.

p. 114 "Bullets were flying . . . of the machine guns." Ibid., p. 389.

p. 114 "As President Roosevelt's son . . . own natural self." http://en.wikipedia.org/wiki/Quentin_Roosevelt

p. 114 "Mrs. Roosevelt . . . break it to her?" Miller, p. 562.

p. 114 "So far as our son . . . small stone put up." Russell, p. 372.

p. 114 "That is a very nice . . . for the great Cause." Robinson, p. 349.

p. 114 "The boy in him had died." Pringle, p. 601.

p. 115 "Yes . . . any other basis." Hagedorn, pp. 381–382.

p. 116 "There was no serious . . . threatened with pneumonia." Robinson, p. 361.

p. 116 "Well, anyway . . . I have done it." Ibid., p. 362.

p. 116 "His face bore . . . weariness in his eyes." Miller, p. 565.

p. 116 "horrid, painful time." O'Toole, p. 403.

p. 116 "Put out the light." Robinson, p. 364.

p. 116 "hollow sound." *New York Times*, January 7, 1919, p. 1.

p. 117 "Theodore, darling!" Miller, p. 566.

p. 117 "The Lion is dead." Hagedorn, p. 386.

14. Remembering Roosevelt

p. 119 "Please accept my . . . shocked me very much." *New York Times*, January 8, 1919, p. 4.

p. 119 "I am shocked . . . a personal loss." Ibid.

p. 119 "the loss of so ardent a supporter of oppressed peoples." Ibid.

p. 119 "With the death . . . nomination for the Presidency." *New York Times*, January 7, 1919, p. 12.

p. 120 "I came . . . best man that ever lived." *New York Times*, January 9, 1919, p. 1.

p. 120 "His country was . . . effective in all our history." Iglehart, pp. 369–371.

p. 120 "He was one . . . history of his country." *New York Times*, January 7, 1919, p. 12.

p. 120 "Yesterday, he seemed . . . bore such a son!" Thayer, p. 454.

SELECTED BIBLIOGRAPHY

Abbott, Lawrence F. *Impressions of Theodore Roosevelt.* Garden City, NY: Doubleday, 1919.

Arizona Republican. December 3, 1902, pp. 1 and 8.

Auchincloss, Louis. *Theodore Roosevelt.* New York: Times/Holt, 2001.

Burrows, Edwin G., and Mike Wallace. *Gotham.* New York: Oxford, 1999.

Charnwood, Lord (Godfrey Benson) *dore Roosevelt.* Boston: Atlantic Monthly Press, 1923.

Chessman, G. Wallace. *Theodore Roosevelt and the Politics of Power.* Boston: Little, Brown, 1969.

Chronicle of America. Mount Kisco, NY: Chronicle Publications, 1989.

Cook, Blanche Wiesen. *Eleanor Roosevelt, Volume One, 1884–1933.* New York: Viking, 1992.

Cooper, Michael L. *Theodore Roosevelt.* New York: Viking, 2009.

Davis, Deborah. *Guest of Honor: Booker T. Washington, Theodore Roosevelt, and the White House Dinner That Shocked a Nation.* New York: Atria/Simon and Schuster, 2012.

Donald, Aida D. *Lion in the White House: A Life of Theodore Roosevelt.* New York: Basic Books, 2007.

Drinker, Frederick E., and Jay Henry Mowbray. *Theodore Roosevelt: His Life and Work.* Washington, DC: National Publishing, 1919.

Gatewood, Willard B. Jr. *Theodore Roosevelt and the Art of Controversy.* Baton Rouge: Louisiana State University, 1970.

The Golden Interlude. Alexandria, Virginia: Time-Life Books, 1969.

Graff, Henry F., ed. *The Presidents.* New York: Scribner's, 1996.

Grondahl, Paul. *I Rose Like a Rocket: The Political Education of Theodore Roosevelt.* New York: Free Press, 2004.

Hagedorn, Hermann. *The Boys' Life of Theodore Roosevelt.* New York: Harper, 1922.

Harbaugh, William Henry. *Power and Responsibility: The Life and Times of Theodore Roosevelt.* New York: Farrar, 1961.

Henderson, Daniel. *Great Heart: The Life Story of Theodore Roosevelt.* New York: Knopf, 1919.

Iglehart, Ferdinand Cowle. *Theodore Roosevelt: The Man as I Knew Him.* New York: Christian Herald, 1919.

Kerr, Joan Paterson. *A Bully Father: Theodore Roosevelt's Letters to His Children.* New York: Random House, 1995.

Lewis, William Draper, introduction by William H. Taft. *The Life of Theodore Roosevelt.* U.S. and Canada: United, 1919.

Lossing, Benson John, ed. *Harper's Encyclopedia of United States History,* 10 Volumes. New York: Harper, 1907.

Lord, Walter. *The Good Years.* New York: Harper, 1960.

Marschall, Rick. *Bully: The Life and Times of Theodore Roosevelt.* Washington, DC: Regnery, 2011.

Martin, James K., Randy Roberts, Steven Mintz, Linda O. McMurry, and James H. Jones. *America and Its People.* New York: HarperCollins, 1989.

McCullough, David. *Mornings on Horseback.* New York: Simon and Schuster, 2001.

McKay, Ernest A. *The Civil War and New York City.* Syracuse, NY: Syracuse University Press, 1990.

McSpadden, J. Walker. *Famous Americans for Young Readers: Theodore Roosevelt.* New York: Barse and Hopkins, 1923.

Miller, Scott. *The President and the Assassin.* New York: Random House, 2011.

Morgan, H. Wayne. *William McKinley and His America.* Syracuse, NY: Syracuse University Press, 1963.

Morgan, James. *Theodore Roosevelt: the Boy and the Man.* New York: Grosset, 1919.

Morris, Edmund. *Colonel Roosevelt.* New York: Random House, 2010.

———*Theodore Rex.* New York: Random House, 2001.

———*The Rise of Theodore Roosevelt.* New York: Coward, McCann, 1979.

Mowry, George E. *The Era of Theodore Roosevelt.* New York: Harper, 1958.

Naylor, Natalie A., Douglas Brinkley, and John Allen Gable. *Theodore Roosevelt: Many-Sided American.* Interlaken, NY: Heart of the Lakes Publishing, 1992.

New York Times, various issues, 1904–1919.

New York Times Book Review, November 18, 2007.

O'Toole, Patricia. *Theodore Roosevelt After the White House*. New York: Simon and Schuster, 2005.

Pringle, Henry F. *Theodore Roosevelt*. New York: Harcourt, 1931.

Riis, Jacob A. *Theodore Roosevelt: The Citizen*. New York: Macmillan, 1904.

Robinson, Corinne Roosevelt. *My Brother Theodore Roosevelt*. New York: Scribner's, 1921.

Roosevelt, Theodore. *The Rough Riders*. Lincoln: University of Nebraska Press, 1998.

Russell, Thomas H. *Life and Work of Theodore Roosevelt*. Homewood Press, 1919.

Stanwood, Edward. *A History of the Presidency from 1897 to 1916*. Boston: Houghton Mifflin, 1916.

Stratemeyer, Edward. *American Boys' Life of Theodore Roosevelt*. Boston: Lee and Shepard, 1904.

Teichmann, Howard. *Alice: The Life and Times of Alice Roosevelt Longworth*. Englewood Cliffs, NJ: Prentice-Hall, 1979.

Thayer, William Roscoe. *Theodore Roosevelt: An Intimate Biography*. New York: Grosset, 1919.

Townsend, Kim, ed. *Manhood at Harvard*. New York: Norton, 1996.

Washington Post, February 16, 1913.

http://www.presidency.ucsb.edu/ws/index.php?pid=29543

PICTURE CREDITS

Banks, Charles Eugene and Armstrong, Leroy. *Theodore Roosevelt: Twenty-Sixth President of the United States: A Typical American.* New York: S. C. Miller, 1901: pages 53, 62.

Famous Americans: Electronic Clip Art. Mineola, NY: Dover, 2005: pages 1, 12 (both) 22, 28, 33, 36 (bottom), 46, 50 (bottom) 54, 57, 72 (both), 82 (top), 93 (bottom).

Hagedorn, Hermann. *The Boys' Life of Theodore Roosevelt.* New York: Harper, 1922: pages 10, 13.

Iglehart, Ferdinand Cowle. *Theodore Roosevelt: The Man As I Knew Him.* New York: Christian Herald, 1919: page 90.

Library of Congress: pages 24, 30, 38, 44, 47, 65, 66, 74, 82 (bottom), 85, 92 (top), 98, 102, 105, 107, 112.

Lossing, Benson John, ed. *Harpers Encyclopedia of United States History.* New York: Harper, 1906: pages 3, 7.

Posters of World Wars I and II Electronic Clip Art. Mineola, NY: Dover, 2006: pages 108, 111.

Russell, Thomas H. *Life and Work of Theodore Roosevelt.* Homewood Press, 1919: pages 113, 118, 121.

Shaw, Albert. *A Cartoon History of Roosevelt's Career.* New York: Review of Reviews, Co., 1910: pages 29, 31, 34, 39, 40, 41, 45, 50 (top), 52, 55, 67, 70, 76, 77, 81, 83, 86, 87, 89, 131.

Scribner's Magazine: pages 11, 16, 19.

Stratemeyer, Edward. *American Boys' Life of Theodore Roosevelt.* Homewood Press, 1919: pages vi, 21, 23, 59.

INDEX